RHODE ISLAND
COURT RECORDS

- 1647-1662 -

Volume #1

Records
of
The Court *of* Trials
of
The Colony
of
Providence Plantations

Southern Historical Press, Inc.
Greenville, South Carolina

Please direct all correspondence and book orders to:

www.southernhistoricalpress.com
or
SOUTHERN HISTORICAL PRESS, Inc.
1071 Park West Blvd.
Greenville, SC   29611

southernhistoricalpress@gmail.com

Originally printed: Providence, RI   1920 & 1922
:ISBN #978-1-63914-660-4

Printed in the United States of America

Preface

With the union of the towns of Portsmouth and Newport in 1640, circuit quarter courts were established, which met alternately in the two towns. The records of most of these sessions are preserved in a manuscript volume entitled "Rhode Island Colony Records 1646-1669," which is in the custody of the Secretary of State. These records have been printed as Chapter XV of the second volume of Chapin's Documentary History of Rhode Island, and cover the years 1641 to 1646. In 1647 the Code of Laws was adopted and the Colony Court of Trials was established, superseding the Island quarter court. This new court was also a circuit court, at first semi-annual, but later quarterly. The records of the greater number of the sessions of this court are preserved in the aforesaid manuscript volume. A transcription of these records has been made and is printed in this volume. The editor wishes to express his appreciation of the courtesy extended to him and his assistants by Hon. J. Fred Parker, Secretary of State, and his staff.

In addition to the Colony Court of Trials, the towns also held monthly courts for the trial of cases which fell within the jurisdiction of these lesser courts.

H. M. C.

Providence,
June, 1920.

RHODE ISLAND COURT RECORDS

Page 35

To Pumham Sachem and to the rest of the Indians to him subject These are to require & charg you & ev of you peaceably to be have yor selves towards or freinds & allyes of Warwick plantacon otherwise calld Showammett offering no injury to them or their goods or cattle & the Like do we Desire & order them to the wards & if any Differences shall arise between ye or any of ye ye shall have a Legall Tryall according to equity and Justice in or Courte when occasion is presented

> Given at this present Court at Nuport 9 of Jun An 1647 The reason of this mandate is a complaint exhibited by the Inhabitants of warwick that they have had some swine killed by the Indians lately wth there plantation

Page 43

Actions Tryed at the General Court of tryals. Houlden at Warwick May the 26: (1649)

JURYMEN

John Greene	Jeames Badcock
Walter Tod	John Briggs
Ezekel Hollima	John Albro
Georg Blisse	nath Dickens
John Wood	will haukins
Robert Griffen	Peter Greene

John Stodder Pll against Tho Gorton in an action uppon the Case for debt & wages Damage layed 5 li: the Jury fine for the Pll: 5 s wages 2 s Damage & the Cost of the Suite Judg granted

John Stodder Pll: against Tho Gorton in an action of assault and battery damage layed 10 li the Jury fine for the

Pll: 1 s Dammage costs of suit: Judgment granted Jeames Barker Plantiff against John Layton in an action of trespas for breach of Covenant damage layed 20 li: Nihil dicit: the Jury fine for the Pll the Defendant to make the Pll an assurance of the land and pay fifty shillings dammage & the Cost of the Suite: the Court granteth Judgment: and execution there uppon:

William Almie Plant against Richard morris in an action upon the cace dammage layed 100 marks refferred untill the next General Court to be houlden at Portsmouth

Thomas Lawton Plant against John Briggs in an action of Slander dammage layed 100 li Demurred untill the next Generall Court to be houlden at Portsmouth

Page 45

JURYMEN

John Green	Je Badc
Walter Tod	John Brigg
E hollyman	J Albro
G Bliss	n Dickens
J Wood	w Haukins
Ro Griff	Pet Gre

At the Court houlden at Warwick from May 26 to the... (1649)

Ralph Erle being Presented for certayne charges in Speeches; traversseth his inditement and putteth himself uppon the tryall the verdict of the Jury is not guilty

for Christopher helmes John Greene put out & Mr. Dyer put in fore man

Christopher Helmes upon the bill presented concerning the death of Rufus Bartin, traversseth his inditement and putteth himself upon the tryall the verdict of the Jury is we finde hime not guilty.

Christopher helmes upon the bill presented concerning the pretended purchase of some of Warwick land traversseth his inditement and putteth himself upon the tryall the verdict of

the Jury is guilty and fine given forty shillings to be payed
into the publick tresurie with in xx Days of the next Session
of Gene Assemblie; Judgment granted and execution thereupon for the charges of the courte

John Warner of Warwick beinge called upon to answer to
some charges by him made against Mr. John Smith President
it was refferred to Mr. Balstone & Mr Houldinge & Phillip
Shearman to and either of them being bound in an Assumpsit
of 100 li apeice to stand to the end these three made

Page 44

At the Generall Courte of Tryall houlden at Warwick from
may the 26 to the 29 (1649)

Jurymen

Jeames Barker	Ralph Erle
Tho lawton	Harcut
Stukly wascot	Carder
Osband	ert Potter
Tho Gorton	[Tho]rniciaft
Christo Helmes	Green

John Layton beinge Called apeared not Richard Harcut Peter
greene & Jeames grene beinge bound over to this Court beinge
Called made thear apearance and weare release and proclaimed quitted.

Robert Taylor & Samuel Goodyer being bound over to this
Court by George Baldwin uppon suspicion of felonie did
travers their inditement and put themselves to be tryed by
god and the Countrie the verdict of the jury is not guilty and
thay are aquitted by Proclamation

It is ordered by this Court that such Cases as are presented
to this Court & putt of untill the next Courte if the Pll: Can
make due proofe that the defendants had lawfull & personall
warninge to apeare at this Court that then the Pll: shall have
his chargis given hime of bringing his actions to this Courte.

Page 12

The Generall Court of Tryalls at Portsmouth: June 26: 1655

Mr. Roger Williams Prsident
Mr. Thomas Olney Asistant for providence
Mr. John Rome Asistant for portsmouth
Mr. Benedict Arnold Asistant for Newport
Mr. Randall Houlden Asistant for warwick
Wm Letherland, Recorder George Parker sargent Capt. John Cranston Atturney
John Greene Soliciter

GRAND INQUEST

Gregorie Dexter	John Gould
Francis Braiton	daniell Gould
wm. havens	tho: Painter
James Weeden Sen.	Stuckle wescoate
Josua Coggeshall	John Greene Jun.
John Briggs	Tho: Stafford

PETITT JURIE

Gregorie Dexter	Daniell Gould
Francis Briton	Tho: Painter
wm Havens	stucle wescoate
James weeden Senr	John Greene Jun
John Coggeshall	Tho: Stafford
John Briggs	John Gould insted
Thomas Brookes	of John Greene

Abner Dedewby beinge bound in a bond of 20 li to his highness to Answare at this Court beinge Called accordinge to order, apeeres not. And soe his bond is Forfuited

James Bawdish apeeringe to prsecute the above saide Abner but he not apeeringe, the said James is freed from his bond.

wm Charles beinge bound by recog ——— the bond of 50 li to apeere at the Court he apeering he is freede from his bond, paying his fees.

The Court adjourned till morninge.

27th: The Court Called.

An action of the Case Comenced by wm. Hall against Richard Burden damage fiftie pounds sterlinge demurred to the next Court of Tryalls the defft paying the present Jury: 18 d pr man. Thomas Laighton & John Andrewes beinge bounde to his highnes in fiftie pounds starling apeece to apeere & according to their bond are by the Court freede from it paying their fees.

An action uppon the Case Comenced by mr wm. Baulston in the behalfe of John hull of Boston, against Ralph Earle senr of Portsmouth damage 50 li sterlinge verdict we finde for the pla, our meaning if the debt of 28 li Expressed in a Covenant bearing date the the 16th septemb (53) damage three pounds marchantable peage by penie white & three per penie black More over Cost of Court, Judgment & Execution granted soe Entred.

An action of of debt by bill Comenced by Capt John Cranston in behalfe of Mr. Wm. Brenton of Boston, against Ralph Earle seyr of Portsmouth, damage 50 li: verdict, we finde for the pla his Bill due of twenty pounds & damage ten pounds at 6 pr penie white, & 3 pr penie black marchantable besides Costs of Court Judgment & Execution granted soe entred.

Richard Burden accused of Asault of Batterie in the Court is by the Jurie Found Guilty & to pay 20 s prsently, & the fees of Court . . .

Ralph Earll sen accused of Batterie in the Court is by the Jurie found Guiltie, & to pay 20 s, prsently, & the Fees of Court.

Page 13

Concerninge the Bonds of mr Holiman for John Gariarde he apeering is dismist as foloweth

In a matter of acusation & Charge Laide against John Gariardy of New-Amsterdam in the New-Netherlands by the Sachims of Naragansitts (vixt) aboute the opeing & Robbinge of a grave of a deceased sister of one of them namely Qus-

suckquangh that wheras the saide Sachims, did uppon foresaide prte noe attaach the goods of the saide John Garriardy
at warwick in this Colonie to the vallue of Fortie seaven
pownds starlinge (he not beinge then prsnally prsent in the
Colonie, and those saide goods or somes of Fortie seaven
pounds, being taken for securitie & Engagement for the saide
John Garriardy his apearance at a Generall Court of Tryalls
in this Colonie, and since tht First Engagement the foresaide
John Gariardy hath Come into this Colonie to attend the
Tryall of the Case prmised & gave in New Bond of Fortie-
seaven pounds for his apearance at this prsent Court hereto
stand to the Tryall of the matter Charged against him, And
Further seeinge the saide John Garriardy hath accordingly
Legally made his apearance at this prsent Court And the
Sachims afore-intended having had notice from the prsident
& from one of the Asistants to Attend this Court & tht heere
they should be heard, & should have Redresse in the matter
of theire Complaints aforesaide if Evedence should be brought
in to prove there Charge, But because non of the saide
Sachims, Either by themselves or by theire Atturneyes or
agents do apeare at this Court to prsecute the Case, or to
Impleade the saide John Garriardy The Court doe therfore
declare that the foresaide John Garriardy is by Law &cr
Cleered from his Bonds & Engagements of Answeringe to this
Court, or any further Attending it in the Case before Prmised.

Page 43

[Court of Trials October 1655]

Mr. Roger williams Prsident
Mr. Tho: Olney Asistant
Mr. John Roome Asistant
Mr. Benedict Arnold Asistant
Mr. Randall Houlden Asistant
Mr. James Barker head warden
wm Lytherland Record.
Capt John Cranston Atturney

Grand Inquest

Richard Burden	John Easton
Henrie Bull	John Cowdall
James Sands	Tho. Painter
John Richmond	Peter Easton
Tho. Cleveton	Obadia Holmes
Josua Coggeshall	Daniell Gould

Itt is by the Court proclaimed tht Thomas Case is Freede from his bonds aboute wm Haviland uppon proclamation Concerninge breach of peace Itt is thought fitt by the Court tht John Parker shall be dismised uppon his subscristion from his bond, aboute breach of peace Concerninge the fines for the Traine band.

The Court ajourned for one houre.

Shuball Painter beinge bound over to the Court & apeering, is by the Court to pay the fees of the Court &.

The Testemonie of mr wm Baulston who saith tht he desired mr Coddington to Record a protest Concerning Capt Rich: moris Jenuarie the 12th 1651, doth now in the prsent Court Testefie his disowinge of tht Record & doth Cleere the said Capt moris uppon tht accompt

Pettitt Jurie

mr wm Jeffrey	Rich: Burden
Lawrence Turner	James Sands
marke Lucar	Josua Coggeshall
Caleb Carr	Rich: morris
Robert Griffin	Tho: Gould
wm woodall	Obadia Holmes

An action of the Case Comenced by Bartholomew agnst John Garriardy uppon damage of 100 li The verdict of the Jurie is tht we find for the pla 50 li & Costs of Court a rehearinge granted Juriemen working: of Providence Henrie Browne, John Feild, & wm Feild, for warwick mr Robert Cole, Rich: Tooy & mr Todd It is ordered by the Court tht for as much as it is Comitted to them the deference betweene

Ralph Earle senr & mr wm Baulston C . . . the saide depending Concerning agst Capt, or John Hull the Court alowes to Ralph Earle aforesaide 15 & the Execution of the former suite to be taken, & soe a Conclusion of the whole matter to prvent all further suits in the Case by Atachments or otherwise

An action Comenced by John Cowdall in an action of debt against John Clawson, verdict, we Find for the pla & give his debt: the Costs of the Court & six pence damage, the debt mr Cowdall damages beinge 33 s.

Judgment Entred.

The Court Ajourned till Eight in the morninge october the 11th the Court Called.

An action of debt uppon an Atachment Comenced by Capt John Cranston against John Elton, uppon damage of 20 li. the verdict we Finde for the pla & give him his debt, Ten shillings damage & the Costs of the Court.

Page 44

tht the Lands in difference betweene them shall be devided by mr nicho: Easton & mr wm Dyre & what charges are uppon tht accompt were equally to be borne. The divisions are to be made by them accordinge to Record & Evidences

Alsoe it is in the power of the above saide James Barker or Richard Tew if they soe meete to ad to the above named mr Easton & mr Dyre Ether mr Roger Williams, mr Benedict Arnold, or mr John Roome, the forenamed Richard Tew acknowleging in Court the True Right of halfe Lobbers pound to belonge to the foresaide James Barker his heirs &.c

JURIEMEN

Rich: Carder	Ralph Earle
These are added to the Former	
wm woodall	beinge taken
Marke Lucker	of . . .

Bartho: Hunt beinge bound over to the peace, the verdict of the Jurie is, we Finde not the bond to be broken

The Court Ajourned til morninge

The Court Findes & order Concerninge defects of Jurie men, Impr: Tho: Olney Junr-10 s: John Browne 10 s: Henrie Fowler 10 s: wm Feild 10 s: John Feild 10 s: mr Todd 10 s: mr Rich: Townsend 5 s. wm woodell 5 s. Nicho: Bivon being Convict of .... Chooses to pay the 5 s. & preideit & beinge Charged for breach of peace uppon his acknowledgment, & prmis of Amendment is by the Court aquitted this was writt againe because of the Last Clause.

An action of Debt uppon accompt Comenced by Capt John Cranston Attorney for Mrs Francis Vaughan, against John Elton uppon an Atachment of his goods uppon damage of Twentie pounds starlinge the verdict we find for the pla & give him his debt, Ten shillings damage & the Costs of the Court Judgment & Execution granted & Entred. mrd tht the Capt Engages that in Case John Elton shall demand a Rehearinge of this Cause wthin or against the next Court wch is in March next then it shall be heard.

George Gardner . . . of his one will pay the . . . of Court . . . standinge . . . verdict.

George Gardner prsented by the Grand Inquest for keepinge John Hicks his wife as his owne Contrarie to Law: The verdict of the Jurie is the pla not havinge made good his Charge, we therefore find for the Defft: damage 6 d. & Cost of the Court, further it beinge proclaimed tht any fine further to pay in it they might be heard but non apeereinge hee was quitt by proclamation

[The following is in the handwriting of Roger Williams]

For as much as the Court hath granted a Rehearing of the Cause betweene John Garriardii & Barth: Hunt: Wm Lytherland Attorney for John Garriardii is bound by Recognizence of Sixtie pound to Bartholo Hunt to prosecute the said Barthol: Hunt at the next: Genr Court of Trialls to be held for this Colon: at Warwick the second Tuesday in March next aproaching:

Wm Vaughan beinge prsented as followeth:

I prsent William Vaughan of Newport for tht Contrarie to

the Law of this Colonie hath taken Mrs. Clarke as his wife

Portsmouth this 26th of June 1655

John **X** Briggs his mark this prsentment beinge found by the Grand Inquest it is Traversd.

The pettitt Juries verdict thereon: as Followeth:

The pla not havinge made good his charge we doe there fore finde for the deffendant: damage six pence, & costs of the Court: wch verdict beinge brought in, An . . . being proclaimed tht if any Could Further accuse or had further to say they might be heard but non apearinge he was quitt by proclamation, in the Court.

The Defft: notwthstandinge, of his owne Free will paide the Costs of Court.

Page 37

The Generall Court of Tryals held at Warwick the 11th of March 1655-56

The Court Called

        Mr. Roger Williams President
        Mr. Tho Olney Assistant
        Mr. John Roome Assistant
        Mr. Benedict Arnold Assistant
        Mr. Randall Houlden Assistant
        Mr. John Greene Sen.
Warwick   Mr. Ezekiell Holiman   Magistrates
        Mr. John Greene Junr
        Wm Lytherland Record
        George Parker Sargent
        Capt. John Cranston Attorney

The court adjourned till next morning

JURIEMEN

Richard Waterman	Joseph Torrey
Mr. John Sanford	John Greene
Thomas Harris	Mr. John Wickes foreman
Tho Roberts wanting	Mr. Henrie Redducke

Mr Wm. Almie   Tho. Layton
Mr John Briggs   Richard Townsend
Samuel Wilbore   James Sweet for Tho R
Obadia Holmes put out

The court adjourned for ½ an houre & then the Commissioners to appeare

The Court ajourned till the Court of Tryalls be over

12th The Court of Tryalls: the Grand Enquest gone forth:

& have brought in there Bills: &c

The Court ajourned for ½ an houre.

The Cause of Bartholomew Hunt & John Garriardy the Isue is not guiltie.

13th Mr. Ezekiell Holiman Engageth tht he will stand to the Condemnation of the Court in the Case betweene Bartholomew Hunt & John Garriardy the verdict: Large & therefore further subscribed

Page 38

The Case between Richard knight pla & Wm Feild defft in an action of the Case for detaining fees &c The verdict is we finde for the defft. & Costs of Court Judgment granted & alsoe Execution.

The action uppon the Case Comenced by Mr Dyre pla against wm Coddington Esqr: uppon damage of 500 li: the Case hath beene much debated & the Result of the Court is that they have taken full Cognisence of the matter & if it shall be proceeded in yett uppon Consideration 5 men tht is mr Samuell Gorton mr John Smith mr John Easton mr John Greene Junr mr Wm Baulston are desired to see if they can compass the matter wch they have done.

obadiah Holmes Jurieman a Case dependinge betweene the state & Caleb Carr, aboute a sheepe tht Tho: Brownell Challengeth, the verdict of the Jurie tht Caleb Carr is cleere.

Bartholemew Hunt beinge desireous to be freede from his Bond of the Last Court after proclamation made he is freede from the Bond paying the Costs thereon. Thomas Brownell accusinge John Coggeshall uppon suspition of Felonie of an Ewe sheepe: he is Bounde uppon 100 li forfeiture to prosecute the saide Josua

Alsoe the said Josua is Bound in the some of 100 li to Answare the complaint at the next Generall Court of Tryalls at Providence.

The Testemonie of Josua Coggeshall saith tht Henrie Bull had the Supina he read it to him, & his Answare was tht he would not goe he would venture the danger.

Tht forasmuch as Henrie Bull of Newport was supinied to apeere at at the next Court apeereinge the Court declare his fine therefore to be Ten pounds to the Gen: Treasurie.

Page 39

[The following item is in the handwriting of Roger Williams]
Mr Lytherland being indicted by Robert Spink for putting his name to a bill without the said Robert Spink his knowledg the Court was satisfied of the weakness of the said R: Spink & of the weakness of his charge & of the innocencie of the said Mr Lytherland & ordered tht he should be cleard by proclamation so accordingly he was

Roger Williams Presidt

The Gen: Atturney Capt: Cranston pleaded the bill before the Court & was satisfied with the proceedings of the Court there being none to prosecute

[Handwriting of Wm. Letherland]

Thomas Robertts fined 10 s for not apeareinge beinge chosen a jurieman.

Capt Richard Moris Comitted beinge acused to be a deliquant & tht soe he stands uppon record wth record acuseth him of Treason &c.

[Handwriting of Roger Williams]
Whereas there have bene differences depending betweene Mr Wm Coddington Esqr. & Mr. Wm Dyre both of Newport

we doe declare—joyntly for orselves & heyres by this present
Record tht a full Agreemt & Conclusion is made betweene us,
by or worthy friends Mr Baulston Mr Gorton Mr John Smith
of Warwick, Mr John Greene junior of Warwick & Mr John
Easton, & in witnes whereof we subscribe our hands & desire
this to be recorded, this present 14 of march 1655-1656

Wm Coddington.

William Dyre.

In the presence of
    Roger Williams presidt
    John **R** Roome
    Benedict Arnold
    John Greene jonir
Wm Coddington & Wm Dyre acknowledg an agreemt in
court March 14th, 1655-56.

Page 47

The Generall Courtt of Tryalls held for the Collony
The 24th of June at providence in the yeare 1656
        Mr. Roger Williams president
        Mr. Tho Olny Assistant
        Mr. William Baulston Assistant
        Mr. John Coggeshall Assistant
        Mr. John Weeckes Assistant
Providence Mr. William Feild   Majestrats
        Mr. Arthur Fenner
        John Sanford Recor
        George Parker Genr Sergant
        Mr. John Easton Generall Aturnie
        Mr. Richard Bulgar Generall Soliciter

THE GRAND JURYMEN

Capt Richd morris foreman	Mr Will Dyre
Mr. Richd Waterman	Mr. Edwd Smyth
Christopher Smyth	Calleb Carr
Thomas Angell	Mr. Joseph Torry
Mr. William Lytherland	Capt Cranston

Richard Knight	Mr Stukly Wascoat
James Sands	Tho Stafford

Thatt upon the Misbehavior of Ralph Earll Senr for sainge in courtt: he would fetch his son outt of the courtt if he pleased: with other misbehaviors: therefor the Court doth commit him to the Custodie of the Generall Sergant

Mrs. Alce Cowland: Beinge Bound to the peace, by Ralph Earll Junr. and for her Apeare to this courtt of Tryals; She is by the court accquited of her bond not seinge any grownds wherefor it should continew: paieinge Fees

JURYMEN

Mr. Ed Smyth	Tho Brownell
Mr. Jo Torry	Calleb Carr
Richard Waterman	Stukly Wastcot
Tho Angell	Tho Stafford
Tho Olny Jur	Chris Smyth
Sam: Bennit	James Ashton

An action of slander & defamation comenced by Richard Morris agst William Coddington damige two hundred pownds starll Genr Issue by the court not guilty The juries verdict, we find for the plaint Eight pownds: damige: and the cost of this court: judgment granted: & execution thereon

An action of the case: Comenced by Mr. William Coddington Esq: plaintiffe against Willia Brenton defendt damige: six hundred pownds: starll

The pla: is non suted for nott apeareinge in Courtt

JURYMEN

Capt Morris foreman	Sam Bennit
Rich Waterman	Tho Brownell
Chris Smyth	Caleb Carr
Tho Angell	Sukly Wastcot
James Sands	Tho Stafford
Tho Olny junr	James Ashton

An action of Trespas: upon the case Comenced by Edward: Richmond plaint against Richard Ussell Defendt Damige one

hundred: pownds starll: The Issue joyned by the Aturnies
not guilty of Trespas: The juries verdict we find for the:
Defendt: the costs of Court: judgment granted and Execution thereon

Ralph Earll junr beinge bound to the peace by Alce Cowland and for his Apearance to this Generall Courtt of Tryals,
he is by the Courtt acquited of his bond paieinge Fees

Mr Richd Burden & Capt Tho Cooke being chosen by the
towne of portsmo. for juriemen & for not apeareinge at the
court we find Each of them tenn shillings

Tho Cleifton beinge by newpt chosen a jurieman & not
apeared is fined tenn shillings

Mr Sam Gorton Senr and mr John Greene Senr beinge
chosen for juriemen for warwicke are fined: each of them
tenn shillings

Page 48

JURYMEN

Smyth	Sam Bennit
J Torry	James Sands
Waterman	Caleb Carr
Chris Smyth	Stu Wastcot
Tho Angell	Tho Stafford
Tho Olny junr	James Ashton

Action comenced by Mr. Wm Brenton pla agst William
Coddington defendt of detenew for detaining certaine certaine
horsis & mares damiges six hundred pownds starll.

Whereas there was fownd in the plaintifs declar A verball
oversight in the word plaint wch should have beine writ defendt the court orders that it may be Rectified according to
the Answer put in by the defendt whoe clearly understood &
Answers according to the scope of it

Upon a longe debate of Mr. Coddingtons demur to this
action, the court orders that the suit shall goe on to Tryall

Mr. William Baulston beinge challenged off the Bench by
Mr. Coddingtons Aturnie did willingly with draw him selfe

The juries verdict is we Find for the plaintife we find sixteene horsis and mares proved upon evidence alive & dead
beside this yeares increase, we find six pence damige & costs
of sute, we find seven liveinge mares and five horsis besides
this yeares increase

Oure judgment is that the defendt shall have the third partt
for keepeinge them judgment granted and exicution thereon

An action of debt Comenced by Mr. William Feild plaintif
agst Ralph Earll Senr damige two hundred pownds starll.
The juries verdict is we find for the plaintife: twenty thre
pownds: deptt due, and twenty shills damige & costs of court
judgment granted: and execution thereon

[Same jurymen]

An Action of Asault and Batterie Comenced by Mr Will
Brenton plaintife agst William Coddington defendt damige
one hundred pownds Starll

This action was withdrawne by the consent of the Aturnies
of boath partts never to be Reniued againe Mr. Coddingtons
Aturnie payinge the jurie & Serjant

An action of Slander and defamation comenced by Ralph
Cowland plaintif agst Ralph Earll Senr Defendt Damige
three hundred pownd Starll

[Same jurymen]

The juries verdict, we find for the plaintife tenn pounds
damige and costs of this court judgment granted and execution thereon

Whereas it was proved in court in the case betwene his
highnes and Joshua Coggeshall there was material evidence
inevitably absent, it is ordered that the persons aforesd shall
continew in there bonds to apeare the next genr court of
Tryals at portsmo provided that this cause shall be the first
cause that shall be heard at the court aforesd.

Finis

Page 54

The Gen Court of Tryals Held for the Collony At portsmouth the 14th of october in the yeare 1656

Grand Jurie

Rich Tew forma
Thom Harris
Rich Waterman
Hugh Bewit
James Badcocke
James Weeden

William Freborne
Daniell Gould
Robt Griffin
Jno Richmond
Will Almy
John Cowdall

Mr Roger Williams president
Mr Tho Olny Assistant for Providence
Mr. Wm Baulston Assistant for Portsmo
Mr John Coggeshall Assistant for newpt
Mr John Weekes Assistant for Warwicke
John Sanford Gen Recordr
Mr Richard Knight Genr Sargant
Mr. John Easton Genr Atturnie
Mr. Richd Bulgar Genr Solicitor
Mr Shereman   Towne Majestrates
Mr Briggs

John Archer and Stephen Wilcocke beinge bound to this court upon Suspetian of Fellony: ar acquitted of these bonds paieinge fees

The Court orderith that whereas there is seized on by Thomas Layton Cunstable of portsmo: the goods of John Andrews to the valleu of five pownds, the saied goods shall be delivered to the saied Andrews

William Morris beinge bownd to this court upon suspetion of Fellony is acquited: paieinge fees

Pettit Jury

Richard Tew: fo: man
Thomas Harris
Rich Waterman
John Greene junr
James Badcocke
Thomas Weeden

Will Freborne
Daniell Gould
Robt Griffen
John Richmond
Will Almy
John Cowdall

An Action of Suspetion off Fellony: Betwene his highness: and Joshua: Coggeshall: The juris verdit is we haveinge noe Inditment accordinge to law our verdit therefore is to leave it to the bench to Detirmaine.

JURYMEN

Rich Tew fo: man	Will Freeborne
Thomas Harris	Phillip Tabor
Rich Waterman	Robert Taylor
John Greene junr	John Richmond
James Badcocke	Willi: Almy
James Weeden	John Cowdall

An action of Trespas upon the case Comenced by Thomas Brownell plaintiff against Joshua Coggeshall deffendt Damige one hundred pownds starll The Genr: Issue the charge is not True. joynd by the Atturnies this caues is Ended by the concents of boath parties in open court

Mr. Brownell: Beinge bound in a hundred pownd forfiture to prosicute Joshua Coggeshall upon suspetion of Fellony is acquited of his bond

An action of Trespas: upon the case for Breach of Covinant and for forcing Abigall Davis the spoused wife of Edward Richmond and for takeing keeping and with houlding her from Edward Richmond aforesaied. Comenced By Edward Richmond plaintiff against John Cowdall and Richard Ussel deffts: damige thre hundred pownds starll

This case is reffered to the court of Comitioners there detirmanation

The case of Mr Coddingtons Reheareinge was Debated by this court And ordered that the case betweene Mr Coddington and Mr Brenton shall be Reheard in the next generall court of Tryalls in the Collony at Newport the next second Tuseday in march next insueinge the first case . . . provided that within tenn daies the tounes of the Collony Disanull not the late court of Comitioners there confirminge of Mr. Coggeshalls Act in the Case Aforesd And that both parties are to take notice hereof without any further sumons

And that Mr Coddingtons Bonds Remaine in full force and vertew

Page 55   .

A Generall Court of Tryalls Held at Newport, march the 10th 1656-57 .

        Mr Roger Williams president
        Mr Thomas Olny Asistant
        Mr William Baulston Asist
        Mr John Coggeshall Asistat
        Mr John Easton Towne Warden
        John Sanford Genr Recor
        Mr Richard Knight Genr Serjant
        Mr John Easton Genr Aturny
        Mr Richard Bulgar Genr Sollisitor

GRAND JURY

Mr John Greene jun'r	Thomas Cornell junr
Mr Thomas Harris	Robert Griffin
Vallintaine Whitman	Edward Thurston
Thomas Walwine	Edward Greeneman
Thomas Cooke Senr	Mathias Harvie
Phillip Tabor	Richard Carder

Ordered that the same authority that Mr Coddingtons Re-hearinge had to be the first case, the same Authority at this present it shall have to be the Second case

PETTIT JURRY

Mr John Greene foreman	Tho Cornell junr
Tho Harris	Robt Griffine
Vall Whitman	Edwd Thurston
Tho Walwine	Edwd Greeneman
Tho Cooke Senr	Mathias Harvie
Phillip Tabor	Richd Carder

Upon a nihill dicet entered by Thomas Hartt pla agst Henry Townsend or his goods or Chatils in an acco of Trespass upon the case for Deteneuer Damidge 20 li starll The jurries verdit we Alow the pla for his princeple and Damidge nine pownds: Sixteene Shills Eight pence, peage six pr peny and cost of Court

Ordered that the Debate of Mr Coddingtons case agst Mr Brenton is Reffered till to morrow morneinge

The Court Resolves about the Rehearinge of Mr Coddingtons and Mr Brentons case that A motion shall be presented from this Court to the next genr Court of Comitionrs, for a meathod and Rule to be given from that Court to this as touchinge a reheareing of causes and summons therein, wherein although thay have granted a Reheareinge, you have not provided a rule and method for us

An Action of Trespas upon the case Comenced by Bartho Hunt pla against John Greene Treasurer for the towne of newport, Deffendt Damidge thirty pownds The jurris verdit is, we find for the Deffendant and alow him Cost of Court

Jury men

John Greene junr foreman	Tho Cornell junr
Tho Harris	Tho Brownell
Vall Whitman	James Badcocke
Tho Walwine	Tho Angell
Tho Cooke Senr	Mathias Harvie
Phillip Tabor	Richd Carder

The opinion of the Court is that the three Ishues Spetified in Mr Will Dyres Declaration against Mr Will: Coddington Trustee and John Greene Trustee and Treasurer for the towne of newport, are thre Distinct actions

An action of Trespas upon the case Comenced by Mr Will Dyre pla against William Coddington Trustee for the towne of Newport and John Greene Trustee and Treasurer for the towne of Newport Deffendt Damidge two hundred pownds starll

The jurris verdit is wee find for the Deffendt & allow him Cost of Court

Whereas Mr Dyre Refused to putt his causes to Tryall

becaues he could not have leagall proceedings in his highnes name. The president publiquly in his highnes name Desired Mr Will Dyre to give in his Reasons to the Court in writinge to which he replied they should have it in print

An Action of Trespas upon the Case Comenced by Will Dyre pla agst William Coddington Defft Damige forty pownds starll

The plaintif refuseinge to putt this case to tryall, the Deffendt by the Courts order Enters a non sute in Court

A presentmen by Mr Richd Bulger genr Sollisitor against Henry persy of portsm for Convayinge & Deliveringe a gun to an Indian, upon the Traverce, the Sd percy apeals to the bench, and is by them acquited paieing fees

Page 56

March the 13th Mr Tho Olny Sits in Court insteed of the president in the case of William Harris his presentment

A presentment by Mr Roger Williams against Will Harris for his open Defieance under his hand agst. our Charter, all our Lawes, & Court the parliment the Lord protector & all government . . . upon the Traverce the Sd Harris pleads not guilty & apeals to God & the Cuntry the jurry beinge impaniled upon the case, proclam was made in open court by o Es three times for A prosicutor but none apeared

JURY MEN

John Greene forema	Tho Cornell junr
Tho Harris	Robt Griffine
Vall Whitman	Peter Easton
Tho Walwine	Jer Willis
Tho Cooke Senr	Mathias Harvie
Phillip Tabor	Richd Carder

A presentment by William Jefferies against Henry Hobsen upon Suspetion of Fellony upon the Traverce the Sd Hobson apeales to God & the Cuntry the jury impanaled, the juries verdit is (Guilty)

A presentment by Mr Richd Bulgar Solisitor agst John Lilly for Sellinge A gunn to an Indian, upon the Traverce the sd Lilly apeales to the Bench. The Result of the Court is that consideringe he was A strainger and alsoe his simpletity this Court petitions to the Court of Comitioners in may next to Release his Find, the sd lily payinge Fees due at this Court

A presentment by Mr Richd Bulgar Solisitor: agst Ralph Earll junr for Asumeinge Authority, upon the Traverce his Father in his steed apeals to the Bench The Court orders that the matter shall be reffered to the next Court of Comrs

A presentment by Mr Roger Williams against Robert West & the wife of Richard Scot Ann Williams and Rebecca Throckmorton, as Comon Aposers of all Authority, the Sd persons apeareinge to Traverce, and none apeared to make good the charge agst them therfore the Court could not proceede further agst them and soe doth accquit them

A presentment by Mr Roger Williams agst Mr Will Coddington as strongly suspected of Contempt of the order of the Collony &cr, upon the traverce there was proclama: made in open three times for A prosicuter, but none apeared, & therfore is acquited payinge Fees

A presentment by Mr Roger Williams against Thomas Gould for Teareinge A protest is by this Court Judged Elegall

It is the opinion of the Court that the presentment against John Smyth and Thomas Hopkins, came not leagally to this Court

Upon the Debate of Richard Chasmor his Tryall the Court orderith that the Saied Chasmore shall be brought to his Tryall to morrow morneinge—beinge Tuseday the 17th Day of this present month march, and therefore Comits him to the Custody of the genr serjant

A presentment by Thomas Harris against Richard Chasemore upon A Comon fame of Buggarie upon the Traverce the Sd Chasemore pleads not guilty and Apeales to god and the Cuntry, the jury impaneled upon the case The jurris verdit whereas Richard Chasemore is here presented for A fame of Buggary we findinge noe Testimony to confirm it our verdit is Not Guilty of the fact

This Court aprehendinge the bond wherein Zackery Rhoads was bound to the Court of Coms Concerninge Chasemore, to be Eleagall, by this Courts Desire Zackery Roades and William Carpenter doe freely in this Court accnowlidge them selves indebted to his highnes the lord protector one hundred pounds starll whereby thay bind them selves that if to any three magistrates in this Collony there doth apeare suffitiant Cause for a new charge in court of Chasemore concerninge buggary by the first of may and the foresaid Zackery Roads and Willie Carpenter soe informed of it within that time under three magistrates hands that then the saied Chasemore shall apeare at our next Genr Court of Tryals exce by some other Authority he be Detained, to Answer to the charg and then this Recognizence to be Voyde

A presentment by Mr Richard Bulgar Generall Sollisitor against Bartholowmew Hunt for not giveinge accompt of two barrils of powder & two hundred pound of lead.

A presentment by Mr Richard Bulgar Solisr against George tute for selinge A picke head to an Indian the sd tute upon the Traverce apeales to the bench and is by them Discharged paieinge Fees

A presentment by Mr Roger Williams against Thomas Harris William Wigenden and Thomas Aingall for Ringeleaders in new devisions in the Collony upon the Traverce the Sd Harris Wigenden and Aingall apeall to the Cuntry for Tryall proclamation beinge made in open Court three times for A prosicutor but none apeared

Robert Griffins presentments against Jeremiah Willis Thomas Gould and Jerimiah Wooly for sellinge liquors by Retaile is by the Court Judged Eleagall.

Page 63

At the Generall Court of Tryalls Held at Warwicke june the 30th 1657.

Mr. Benidict Arnold presidtt
Mr William Baulston Asistant
Mr Richard Tew Asist
Mr Randall Houldon Assistant
Mr. Ezeckill Holyman
Mr Walter Todd   Towne Majestrats
John: Sanford Genr Recor
Mr Richard Knight Genr Serjant

Grand Jurymen

Mr John porter foreman	John Richmond Senr
Mr James Greene	Amos Wastcott
Mr Mathias Harvie	Thomas Stafford
John Smyth Mason	William Burton
Robert Wastcot	James Sweet
Thomas Relph	John Lipitt senr
Mr Joseph Clarke	

Pettit Jury

Mr John porter foreman	Mr Joseph Clark
Mr James Greene	Amos Wastcott
Mr Mathias Harvie	Thomas Stafford
John Smyth Mason	William Burton
Robert Wastcott	James Sweet
Thomas Relph	John Lipitt senr

An action of the case to answer the Condemnation of the Court upon A nihil dicett Entered before the Court of Tryalls in october last at portsmo, Comenced by Edward Richmond plaintiff against Richard Ussell Deffendant Damidge Forty pownds starll jurries verdit we Find for the plaintiffe Damidge sixe pownd and Cost of this present Court judgment granted and exicution thereon

Christopher Smyth chosen for A jurry man By the towne of providence is Remitted his fine by Reason of the weaknes of his body

Richard Sison chosen jurry-man for portsmouth his Famely

beinge Sicke and Ill and haveinge none to atend them but him selfe his fine is Remitted

Nicholas power and Roger Moory chosen jurry men by the towne of providence they not atendinge nor makeinge their Exscuse are Fined Each of them tenn shillings

James Sands: chosen jurry-man for portsmouth, and he not atending is fined tenn shi

Toby Sanders and John Greene chosen jurry-men for Newport, and they not atendinge the court are Fined Each of them tenn Shillings

Thomas Greene of Warwicke haveinge spoaken Contemptious words in and to the Court and Refuseinge to make his acknowlidgment, the sayd Thomas Greene is bound in A bond of tenn pownd starll: Forfiture to answer it at the next generall Court of Tryalls, and upon the Same penalty to be of A peaceable behaviour in the mean-time

This bond was Taken in Court and Red in his heareinge

It is ordered that the generall Recorder shall graunt Forth Sumons to the generall Serjant to Sumon Henry Hobson of Newport to apeare at the next generall Court of Tryalls there to answer the verdit of jurry: at the last generall Court of tryalls held at newport in march last

Whereas Mr Samuell Gorton was fined at the Genr Court of Tryalls held at provid in june 1656 his fine is by this court remitted

Francis Durby bein ingadged Testifyeth that he is in Feare of his life from Robert Wastcot and Jerimiah Wastcot Taken in Court Robert Wastcot and jerimiah Wastcot are bound in A bond of tenn pownds starll Forfiture to answer the complaynt of Francis Durby at the next generall Court of Tryalls held for the Collony the second Tuseday in october next at providence, and in the meanetime to be of A peaceable and quiat behaviour to all men upon the forfiture aforesayd

This bond was Taken and Red to the parties in Court

Francis Durby is bound in A bond of tenn pownds Forfiture to prosicute Robert Wastcott and Jerimiah Wastcott: for Breach of the peace at the next generall Court of Tryalls held for the Collony the Second Tuse-day in october next at providence

Mr John Smyth and Mr John Weecks chosen jurry-men by the towne of Warwicke and they not atendinge the Court are fined Each of them tenn Shills

Page 64

Att the Generall Court of Tryalls held for the Collony at providence the 13th octobr 1657

   Mr Benedict Arnold presidtt
   Mr Arthur Fenner Asistant
   Mr William Baulston Asistant
   Mr Richard Tew Asistant
   Mr Randall Houldon Asistant
   Mr William Feild
   Mr Henry Browne Towne Magestrates
   John Sanford Genr Recor
   Richard Knight Genr Serjant
   Mr John Greene junr Genr Aturny

GRAND INQUEST

Mr John Easton foerman	Phillip Tabor
Thomas Aingall	Thomas Layton
Vallintine Whitman	Robert Griffin
Edward Enman	Thomas Greene
Stephen Wilcocke	Amos Westcot
Richard Bulgar	Richard Carder

PETTITT JURRY

Mr John Easton foreman	Thomas Hopkins
Thomas Aingall	Thomas Layton
Vallintine Whitman	Thomas Greene
Edward Enman	Amos Westcott
Stephen Wilcock	Richard Carder
Richard Bulgar	

An Action of Trespas upon the case comenced By Abigall Davis pla: against Richard Ussell Defftt: Damidge tenn pounds starll:

The Issue joyned by the Aturnie is the Defft knows noe Abigall Davis of newport and the Deft is not guilty of the charge

The jurry cominge into the Court did Declare that they cannot Agree to bringe in A verdict and will noe longer atend upon the case

That whereas ther were two actions comenced by Mr Samuell Smyth of Conetticott in the behalfe and for Debts Due to John Stadder and Luke Hitchcocke boath of Connetticott aforsd against William Feild and also two actions comenced by Mr Richard Lord and Mr Samuel Smyth aforsayd: against Mr Randall Houldon And Mr John Smyth and partners:—The parties contendinge have Refferred som chargis to the vallew of twenty and alsoe one Ewe lambe beinge in Difference between them, to the judgment and Detirmination of the Bench the Remainder of what was due beinge Ended by Compromise by the parties them selves.

Providence Oct 15, 1657

Memorandum: Wher: as ther hath beine Reffered into the Court of Tryalls now in Beinge to put an End and give Detirmination to a Difference that Remained between Mr Samuell Smyth of Wethersfeild &cr and Mr William: Feild Mr John Smyth of (Warwicke) Mr Houlden &cr of this Collony, which difference was A Demaund of twenty pownd, And A Ewe lambe, by the afor-named Mr Samuell Smyth, of the afor-named Feild &cr for charge of Fetchinge paymente and for Non-payment of fower Ewes one yeare, we have taken into serious consideration the premises and have seriously weighed the alligations, on both parts, and upon the same Considerations doe unanimosly agree, that provided the afor-named William Feild and partners, doe make good and performe, unto the afor-named Samuell Smyth all other their late agreement and acknowledgments as agreed by them concerned the late greivencies or actions Comenced by him the

sayd Smyth against them, Then for A Fynall conclusion Issueinge and Endinge all Differences betweene the parties afor-
sayd the Court doe Award and declare, concerninge the
twenty pownd the Ewe lamb in Difference and Reffered, that
Mr Feild and partners shall pay unto the afor-named Sam
Smyth &cr twelve pownd in pay Equivolent to Ewe sheep at
forty shills a pece and also shall to him Deliver, one ewe
lamb in or within the time, that they have agreed to pay their
other Dues to the sayd Smyth, and this result and award we
make and give in the premisis, by vertue of A Mutuall consent of both the abov-named Samuell Smyth and William
Feild &cr in the face of the court vollenterily Refferinge the
Differences to the Courts Result and Detirmination to testify
the Courts joynt agreement in the premisis it is Subscribed

          Benidict Arnold presidtt
          Arthur Fenner Genr Asistant
          William Baulston Genr Asistant
          Richard Tew Genr Asistant
          Henry Browne Deputy
             of the Towne providence

Memorand: that after the Court had made the detirmination Abovsayd, the abov-named William Feild & partners
with him gave to the abov-named Samuell Smyth &cr Spetially
under their hands for payment of A certain or certaine sums
in September next, in which sum or sums is comprehended
the twelve pownd and the Ewe lamb abov-mentioned
Witnes us herto subscribinge this 16th Octor 1657

          Richard Tew Genr Asistant
          John Easton
          John Greene junior

In answer and upon the Request of Mr William Feild Mr
Randall Houldon and partners, this Court have constituted
and apoynted Mr Benidict Arnold presidt, Mr Samuell Gorton Mr John Easton and John Sanford to be an Awditt to
heare accompts between them which concerne matters of
Trancactions Debts and payments in partner-ship, in shiping
and things from that ariseinge, and that what the sayd Awditt

or the Major part of them shall Detirmin, thereupon, shall be Faythfully performed by Each party and that the Sayd Awditt shall meett togather for Issueinge the Sayd Bussinis on the 10th of Novembr next at the Dwelling house of Mr Baulston in portsmouth, And if any person shall neglect to performe what the Awditt shall Detirmin his Due to pay, it shall be lawfull for the greived party to take Forth Execution to take of the Estat of the party wronging in the premisis, for satisfaction to the party wronged—

This order is consented to by Mr Houldon & partners as A judgment acknowlidged in Court

Page 65

That wheras Robert Griffin did in the Face of the Court and out of the Court before . . . carry him self very usively to the great Desturbance of many and also for his Cont. . . . . in the Court toward the bench, the Court have therfor Comitted the sayd Griffin to the . . . of the genr Serjant duringe the Courts sitting to prevent further Disturbance for as much as untill he was comitted the Court could not Sitt in quiat notwithstanding all fayre perswasions to Restraine him—

Thomas Layton of portsmo: being presented for Denying certaine persons belonginge to the towne of portsmo of their share of powder contrary to order—

The Court not Finding it the breach of any law in the Collony have cast out the bill

Wheras ther was A presentment by Marke Lucker by order of the Trustees of the towne Newport against William Dyre of Newport and ther beinge the want of A Tittle in the word senior the Court have ordered that the sayd bill shall be Returned, to the sayd Marke Lucker againe, for that William Dyre Reffused to answer the presentment therupon Whereas ther was one Arthur Venner of providence presented by Roger Williams and sumons goeing forth, the serjant hath dilligantly serjant the Collony and cannot find any of that name

Whereas ther was A presentment against John Mose of portsmo, by Robert Griffin the Court doe judg it came not leagally to the Court

Whereas ther was A presentment against Gregory Dexter of providence by Roger Williams presidt of providence for beinge Ringleader in New divisions in the Collony, and Mr Roger Williams not apearing to prosicute the sayd Gregory Dexter is to be cleared by proclamation payinge Fees

Wheras ther was A presentment by Mr Roger Williams, against John Sayles and Samuell Bennit of providence, for being Ringleaders in New divisions in the Collony and the accuser not apearinge, the sayd parties are to be cleared by proclamation paying Fees

Wheras ther are Severall presentments hanging upon Fyle and the parties therein presented have beine sumoned to answer the presentments and they not apearinge, it is ordered that the Genr Aturney shall present the matter to the next Court of Comitioners for their Result therin

Ordered that wheras Henry Hobson of Newport was sumoned to apeare at this Court and he not apearing, this Court have ordered, that sumons shall goe Forth againe, to sumons the sayd Hobson to answer, the verdit of jurry at the last Court of Tryalls at Newport, at the next genr Court held at portsmo, alsoe the Court have Recomended his contempt in not apearing according to sumons, to the Genr Aturny for Further progress therin—

Wheras Hugh Bewitt late of providence and Thomas Winterton of Newport were bownd by Recognizence to apeare at this Court, and thay Forfitting their Recognizence by non apearance, this Court doe order that Exicution shall goe Forth upon the Estates of the sayd parties according to the Contents of their Bonds

Whereas Thomas Green was bound to this Court and to the good behavior, the sayd Thomas Green is by the Court Freed from the sayd bonds by proclamation having payd Fees

Whereas Robert Westcott and Jerimiah Westcott were at the last Court, bownd to this Court and to the good behaviour, they are by their Court cleared by proclamation paying Fees

Itt is ordered by this court as touching Robert Griffins Rescuinge A prisoner in Newport together with other contemptious cariages that he be bownd to the next Court of Tryalls at portsmouth and in the mean time to be bownd in A bond of five pownd to his good behavior.

Therfor, yow Robert Griffin are bownd to his highnes the lord protector in A bond of Five pownd to your peacabl behavior towards all his highness subjects in this Collony during this and the next Court of Tryalls to be holden at portsmouth wher you are to Apeare to make Answer for Rescuing A prisoner, with other Contemptious Carriages:—

Taken and Red to the party in Court

Capt: Thomas Cooke chosen jurry-man by the towne portsmouth, & he not atending is by the Court Fined tenn shillings

Mr John Coggeshall chosen jurry-man by the towne Newport, & he not atendinge is Fined tenn shillings

Henry Bull chosen jurry-man by towne Newport, & he being lame his Fine is by the court Remitted

Page 66

Att the Genr Court of Tryalls held for the Collony at Portsmouth

March: the 9th 1657-58

>   Mr Benidict Arnold president
>   Mr Arthur Fenner Asistant
>   Mr William Baulston Asistant
>   Mr Richard Tew Asistant
>   Mr Randall Houldon Asistant
>   Mr John Brigs   Wardens for
>   Mr William Freeborne   portsmo
>   John Sanford: Genr Recor
>   Richard: Knight Genr Serjant
>   Mr John Greene junr Genr Atturny

GRAND JURRY-MEN

Mr Edward Smyth fore-man   peter Greene
Edward Enman   James Sweete

Captn Thomas Cooke	Amoss Wascote
James Badcocke	Samuell Wilbore
Thomas Layton	peeter Easton
John Easton	Lott Strainge
Henry Bull	

Bartholowmew West Beinge Bownd to this Court to prosi-cute his mayd he haveinge Apeared at this Court is By this Court acquitted: of his Bonds

Robert Griffin Beinge By Recognizence Bownd to this Court, And by the Generall Aturny Indicted for an affray, By Disorderly and Extravigant Caridges acted at Thomas Goulds house on the 6th of January 1657 The jury impanelled

Upon the Traverce, he pleads not guilt: and Reffers him Selfe to god and the Cuntry for Tryall

PETTITT JURRY

Mr John Easton foreman	Henry Bull
Edwd Enman	petter Greene
Captn Tho Cooke	Sam Wilbore
James Badcocke	Francis Brayton
Thomas Layton	Lott Strainge
Mr petter Easton	John Almy

Thomas Gould Beinge By Rekognizence Bownd to this Court, And by the Genr Aturny indicted for an afray: by Disorderly cariadges acted in his house the 6th: of January: 1657 The jurry impanelled: Upon the Traverce he pleads not guilty: And Reffers him Self to god and the Cuntry for Tryall

Thomas Winterton Beinge by Recognizence Bownd to this Court And by the Genr Aturny indicted For A: Fray by Dis-orderly cariadges, acted in and at Thomas Goulds howse on the 6th of Janury (1657) The jury impanelled: Upon the Traverce pleads not guilty & Referrs him Selfe to god and the Cuntry for Tryall

Edmund Audly Beinge by Recognizence bownd to this Court and the Genrl Aturny indicted for an afray by Disorderly Carriadges, acted in & at Thomas Goulds house the 6th of

January 1657 The jurry impanelled: upon the Traverce pleads not guilty and Referrs him Selfe to god and the Cuntry for Tryall

John Sheldon Beinge by Recognzence bownd to this Court and by the Genrl Aturny indicted for an afray by Disorderly Carridges acted in and at Thomas Goulds howse on the 6th janr 1657 The jurry impanelled: upon the Traverce pleads not guilty And refferrs him Selfe to god and Cuntry for Tryall

The jurry returned and their answer is that the indictments came not Soe orderly to them as to justify them to give in A verditt because it had not beine passed on by A grand in quest before hand

Thomas Gould Robert Griffin Edmund Audly John Sheldon and Thomas Winterton all of newptt Beinge bownd over to this Court for Disorders Done at Thomas Goulds house on Wedensday night the sixt of january last and the Court haveinge had A verry strict and a Searious hereinge and inquiry into the matter are convinced that the sayd persons in their then drinkinge helths intended nothinge against the dignity of his highnes the lord protector, &cr thay also Solemly Denyinge any indignity intended in the same, and also confesinge their sorrow for their Rude and unorderly Caridges at the afore-sayd time and place, and of makeinge soe much disturbance therby and promisinge every one of them to Endeavour to avoyd the licke Disorderly actions againe, the Court are pleased noe longer to continue the sayd persons to stand bownd but upon payinge Fees due to officers of Court thay are Discharged by proclomation in open Court

Wheras Robert griffin was at the last Court at providence bownd to this Court and was then bownd to the good behaviour he haveinge apearred in this Court is by the court acquitted and cleared by proclama in open Court

Lawrence Turner beinge bownd for Richard Ussells apearance the last Genrl Court of Tryalls held at providence in octor last to answer the complaynt of Abigall Davice in an action of Trespas upon the case &cr, and the sayd Uzzell makeinge then his apearance according to law, the Court doe Declare Turners bond to be voyde for the forsayd Reason but doe not acquit or justify the jurry impanelled on that case for that thay did not breinge in A verdict thereupon

Whereas Henry Hobson was sumoned to this Court to answer the Condemnation of the verdict of jurry at the Genrl Court held at newport in march last the matter is reffered to the Court of Comissioners

Henry Tibbots being bownd to the Court and presented by Henry Hobson . . . The jury impanelled on this case

Page 67

The jury impanelled on the Case. Upon the Traverce pleads not Guilty and refers him Selfe to god and the Cuntry for Tryall The juris verdict (Not Guilty) whereupon Henry Tibbots is acquitted by proclamation paying Fees

John Easton foreman	peetter Greene
Edwd Enman	Sam Wilbore
Capt Tho Cooke	Francis Brayton
James Badcocke	peetter Easton
Tho Layton	Lott Strainge
Hen: Bull	John Almy

PETTITT JURRY

Mr Hen: Bull foreman	Sam Wilbore
Edwd Enman	Francis Brayton
Captn Tho Cooke	James Sweete
James Badcocke	Lott Strainge
Tho Layton	John Almy
peetter Greene	Amoss Westcot

Robert Spincke beinge Bownd to this Court and presented by Henry Hobson in A Charge of Fellony The jurry impanelled on the Case

Upon the Traverce pleads not Guilty and reffers him Selfe to god and the Cuntry for Tryall The jurris verdict (Not Guilty) whereupon Robert Spincke is acquited by proclama payinge Fees

Henry Hobson indicted by the Genrl Aturny for Contempt of Authority for Refuseinge to apeere at the Court held at providence, accordinge to sumons

The jurry impanelled on the Case

Upon the Traverce pleads not Guilty & Reffers him Selfe to god and the Cuntry for Tryall The juries Verdict is (Guilty) Whereupon Henry Hobson is bownd to the peace & good behavior

You Henry Hobson doth ow and stand indebted unto his highnes the Lord protector of England &cr the full & just sum of five pownds starll to be levied on yor goods or chattills The condition of this bond is that if the above bownden Henry Hobson shall be of A quiat and peacable behavior to all his highnes subjects. Dureinge this and the next Genrl Court of Tryalls held for the Collony the last Tuseday in june next at newport as also at that Court to make your personall apearance then this obligation to be voyd otherwise to stand in Full Force and vertue

Wheras William Carpenter and Zachery Roades were chossen jurry-men by the towne of providence and thay not servinge their Fines are Refferred to the next Genrl Court of Tryalls: Foras much as there is probability that there will be adjetation of the matter amonge the Court of Comissioners

Page 75

The Genrl Court of Tryalls Held for the Collony at Newport on the . . . Day of June 1658

        Mr: Benidict Arnold president
        Mr William Feild Asistant
        Mr William Baulston Asistant
        Mr Joseph Clarke Asistant
        Mr Randall Howldon Asistant
        Mr William Jeffery } Wardens for
        Mr Edward Smyth } Newport
        John Sanford Genrl Recordr

Richard Knight Genrl Serjant
Mr John Greene junr Genrl Aturny

GRAND JURRY MEN

Mr James Barker foreman	John Archar
Joseph Torry	John Crandall
John Cowdall	James Rogers
Benja Herndall	Thomas Hedger
Caleb Carr	Robert Westcot
William Earll	Lawrence Turner

PETTIT JURRY

Mr Jos: Torry foreman	John Crandall
Mr John Cowdall	James Rogers
Benj: Herndall	Tho :Hedger
Willi Earll	John pepody
John Archar	Robert Westcott
Caleb Carr	Richard Card :

An Action of the Case for Debt Comenced by Henry Tib-
bots plaintiff against Henry Hobson Defendant Damidge
Twenty pownds : The Genrl Ishue joyned by the Aturnies not
Guilty

Juries verdict we find for the plaintiff tenn pownds starll
two pence damadg and Cost of Court

Judgment graunted

PETTITT JURRY

Mr James Barker foreman	John Crandall
Ben: Herndall	James Rogers
Jos: Torry	John pepody
Willi: Earll	Tho Hedger
John Archar	Rich Card :
Caleb Carr	Richard Carder

An Action of the Case for Trespas done Comenced by John
Cowdall plaintiff against Thomas paynte[r] Deffendant Damadge Fifty pownds The Genrl Ishue Entered by the Aturnies

is not Guilty of Trespas   The juries verdict we finde for the plaintiff twenty shills Damadge and the Costs of Court judgment Entered:

Upon ajetation with Samuell Crooke in the Court to Compose the matters of Difference between Robert Westcot and him: the sayd Crooke sayd he would work it out, But Sayth he in the Court who: so-ever takeith me Servant I will be the Death of him or he shall be the Death of me upon which he had the locke put on his lege againe and Robert Westcot proceeded to Tryall

An Action of Dept Commenced By Stukely Westcott plaintiff against Samuell Crooke deffendant   Damadge: 10 li: upon the sayd action beinge called in Court The Defendt Doth acknowlidge judgment for 1 li: 13s. 9d. debt to Stukely Westcot after the Rate of peage 8 pr peny: judgmt graunted

An Action of Debt Commenced by Robert Westcott plaintiff against Samuell Crooke Deffendant   Damadge twenty pownds: upon the Action beinge called the Deffendant doth acknowlidge the debt of 2 li: 18 sh: to Robert Westcot peage 8 pr peny: and ownes judgment against him in boath these actions for boath the Sayd Sumes provided this may be noe damadge unto him the sayd Crooke in any other differences between the afor-sayd Stukely Westcott and him: judgment graunted

PETTIT JURRY

Mr James Barker foreman	John Crandall
Benj: Herndall	John Cowdall
Willi. Earll	Tho: Hedger
John Archar	Ema: Wooly
Caleb Carr	Richard Card
John pepody	Richard Carder

An Action of the Case for Trespas comenced by Joseph Torry plaintiff against George Bliss deffend   Damidge twenty pownds: The Genrl Ishue joyned by the Aturnies Not Guilty

The juries Verdict We finde for the plaintiff Five pownds Damadge and the Costs of Court

Judgment graunted: The Deffendant accordinge to law hath payd the vallew of the Bill of Costs and therby Stopes Exicution, to have the action Reheard at the next Genrl Court of Tryalls

PETTIT JURY

Mr Jam: Barker foreman	John Crandall
Benj Herndall	John Cowdall
William Earll	Tho Hedger
John Archar	Eman: Wooly
Tobi Saunders	Richard Card
John pepody	Richard Carder

A presentment by Henry Hobson: pla: Against Henry Tibbotts for Fellonious Takeinge away six Ewe goates from the Sayd Hobson: The Deffendant Enters his Traverce pleads not guilty and Reffers him Selfe to god and the Cuntry for Tryall: The jurry impanelled The jurries Verdict (We Find not Guilty) Whereupon Henry Tibbotts is cleared by proclamation in open Court payinge Fees

The Court doe Agree and order, that Henry Tibbotts Goates beinge Sixe Ewes and their increase beinge in the Custody of James Man late Cunstable of Newport who by order tooke them and was ingadged to secure them untill it were tryed whither he the sayd Tibbotts had Felloniously Taken the Sayd Goates or noe: And he beinge fownd not Guilty by the judgment of his peeres at this Court, Therefore the Court doe order that the Genrl Recorder shall give forth order unto Edward Thurston Cunstable of Newport to Demaund and Receive the sayd Goates of the sayd James Man and to Deliver the Sayd Goates unto the Sayd Henry Tibbotts and that from this pressent Court.

It is ordered that the Genrl Recorder doe give forth order from this court unto James Man late Cunstable of Newport to Deliver the hatt to Henry Tibbots which was Taken by

warrent of search out of Robert Spincks howse it beinge
cleared that the Hatt is the sayd Henry Tibbotts

Roger Williams of portsmouth doth owne him Selfe indebted unto his highnes the lord protector of the comon welth
of England &cr the Full and just sum of tenn pownds starll:
to levied on his goods or chattills &cr   The condision wherof
are that if the sayd Roger Williams shall breinge in and Deliver to the Court when they shall please to call for it: A Gunn
Which now is in Controvercy and Delivered in the Court to
the sayd Williams then his Bond to voyd, otherwise to stand
in full force and Vertue

Page 76

A presentment by the Genrl Aturny Against Francis Durby
for Breach of the peace by Asault &cr   The Deffendant enters
his Traverce: pleads Guilty and Reffers him Selfe to the
Bench for Tryall   Wherupon the Court doe order that Francis Durby shall pay five shills for the Breach of the peace to
the Genrl Treasurer: And doth promise to be of A peaceable
Behavior towards Sarah Herington and to forbare cominge
to her mothers howse and this to be of Force untill the majestrates of the Towne of Warwicke shall see Cause to cleere him.

And is in the Court Acquitted from his former Bonds by
proclamation in Court payinge Fees

A presentment By the Genrl Aturny against Samuell Crooke
for giveing Contemptious Speeches against the Government:
The Defendt enters his Traverc: pleads Guilty: and Refers
him Selfe to the Bench for Tryall

Samuell Crooke being Examined in Court whether he knew
of any law in the Massachusetts which did forbid A
majestrate from medlinge with A Massachusett man heere:
he Answered noe: and sayd: that he was mad or unadvised
in soe sayinge: And that he did not know that the majestrates
here were disorderly men and what he sayd was upon A rumor
and not upon his owne knowlidge: and that he is sorry for
thosse expressions

Wherupon the Court doe order that Samuell Crooke is

Bownd in A Bond of Five pownds to be of A peaceable and quiet Behaviour Dureing this and the next Genrl Court of Tryalls to be held at Warwicke and is acquitted of his Former Bonds payinge Fees

A presentment by Richard Knight against Samuell Crooke for Breakinge prison and Takeinge away goods: The Deffendt, Enters his Traverce: pleads Guilty: and Refers him Selfe to the Bench for Tryall. The Court upon the acknowlidgment of the sayd Crooke of the Courts Favour and his unworthyness therof he is acquitted payinge Fees:

Henry Hobson Beinge Bownd to this Court and to the good behavior: is acquitted by procla- payinge Fees

Upon A case Against Anthony parrent who stands Bownd to this Court in A Bond of Forty pownds to Answer matters of very pernitious nature against the peace of the place: yett noe perticuler law beinge Fownd that is of Force in the Collony which Takeith hould of the Sayd offence untill accordinge to Genrl Courts order the Genrl Councell be called together to search the lawes of England as touchinge the premises: and to that end the Court so Cause that the president give Forth his Warrant for the Genrl Councell to Asemble at Warwicke the second Tuseday in october next for that purpose Therfor Anthony parrent stands Bownd in the Bond of Forty pownd untill the next Genrl Court of Tryalls held at Warwicke the Second Tuseday in october next then and ther to Answer what shall be aledged against him as concerninge the sayd charges:

Wheras Coginaquont an Indian Sacham was Bownd in A Bond of Tenn pownd to breinge in the Body of an Indian named Casseejuwasuck into this present Court to answer William Bayly for Forceable takeinge away his goods: And the sayd Casseejuasuck beinge caled in Court and not Apeereinge the Court doe Declare that the Sayd Cogainaquont hath Forfitedt the Sayd Bond and Sum of tenn pownds which sayd sum shall be payd as Followith viztt To the Towne of Newport for keepeinge the sayd indian thre pownds fowerteen shills to the Genrl Recorder tenn shills eight pence and fower pownds shall be payd into the Genrl Treasury: And the Sum of one pownds fifteene shills fower pence to William Bayly afor-Sayd who was Bownd to this Court to prossicute the sayd indian Casseejuwasuke who not apeareinge the sayd Bayly is acquitted from the sayd Bond:

Upon A presentment by the Grand Jurry against Edward Richmond for liveinge with Abigall Davise contrary to the law of this Collony: The Deffendant Enters his Traverce: pleads Guilty Soe Far as he lives Contrary to law: And Reffers him Self to the Bench for Tryall: The Court doe judge the Sayd Edward Richmond Guilty of Fornication and to be whipt or pay Forty Shills accordinge to law: The sayd Edward Richmond Doth acknowlidge to abide the law in payment of Forty shills to the Genrl Treasurer: judgment graunted

Upon A presentment by the Grand jurry against Abigall Davice for liveinge with Edward Richmond contrary to the law of this Collony: The Defendant Enters her Traverce: pleads Guilty and Reffers her Selfe to the Bench for Tryall: She also in Court owned herselfe to be the same woman Abigall Davice: and that she hath a chylde by Edward Richmond   The Court doe judge her Guilty of Fornication: and to be whipt or pay Forty shillings—accordinge to law: She ownes to abide the law in payment of Forty shills to the Genrl Treasurer   Judgment Granted:

Upon the humble Request of Edward Richmond and the aforementioned Abigall Davice that thay haveing beine adjudged: and also thay owneinge the Righteousnes of the Sentence of the Court against them for liveinge together in Fornication: That now this Court would be pleassed for prevention of the licke Temptation now to Declare them Selves Condissendinge to the two parties marriag to gether: which the Court doe Consent unto: for that ther is Testimony that they have beine twice published according to law but that Mr Jeffery advised them to stay A litle while becaus obadyah Holmes Forbad it thoe he shewed noe Reason nor hath accordinge to law proceeded in the matter since therefor the Court Declares under the hands of the Court or by their names herto anexed that the sayd persons are married together before and in pressents of the Court Leagaly

Ben: Arnold prsdt	Randall Howldon Asist
William Baulston	Will Jefferay
Joseph Clarke	John Greene Aturny Genrl

Mary paull the Daughter of John Richmond of Newpt Senr. beinge Examined Confessith that she was with chyld by Richard Canterbury before she was married: Wherupon John Richmond and the sayd mary are bownd in A Bond of Fower pownds: that the sayd mary shall make her lawfull apeareance by her Selfe or her Aturny at the next Genrl Court of Tryalls held at Warwicke ther to abide the detirmina of the court for Fornication

Ordered that Mr Gregory Dexter for not atending the jury is fined 10 s: and Edward Smyth 5s: beinge both of providence: and William Woodell and Lott Strainge are fined each 10 s: for not atendinge the jury

[last line on page torn away
and James Greene and Thomas Greene are fined each 10 s.]

Page 80

The Generall Court of Tryalls Held at Warwicke the 16th of octobr: 1658

> Mr Benedict Arnold pressident
> Mr William Feild Asistant
> Mr William Baulston Asistant
> Mr Joseph Clarke Asistant
> Mr Rundall Houldon Asistant
> Mr Ezechill Holyman } Deputies for Warwicke
> Mr John Greene junr }
> John Sanford Genrl Recor
> Richard Knight Genrl Serjant
> Mr John Greene junr Genrl Aturny

GRAND INQUEST

Joseph Torry Foreman	Thomas Greene

Caleb Carr	christo: Almy
George Bliss	John Lippitt senr
Richard Carder	John Sweete
Thomas Relph	Thomas Bradlie
James Greene	John Gerriardy

The Grand Jurry impanelled and sent Forth

The Grand jurry returned and say they have Nothinge to breinge to the Court

Ordered that the Genrl Treasurer shall pay twelve shillings to Samuell stafford for his journie to providence upon the Collonies occasion:

Whereas Nicholas power of providence was Fined at the Generall Court of Tryalls for not atendinge as A jurry man and it now apeareinge to this Court by Testimony that the sayd power was sicke at that time and could not attend the Court It is Therfore ordered that his Fine is remitted

Foras much as it pleassed the devine providence by Contrary windes and other impediments to hinder severall persons from atendinge this pressent Court who had actions Dependinge in this Court and Som others who by bond or ingadgement to make their apeareance here: The court conceive and conclude it nessisary, and of absolute nesessity therefore to adjourne this pressent Court untill the First wedensday in November now next insueinge, that soe such persons as are concerned may save their Bonds by makeinge their lawfull apearances at this Court at Warwicke then to proceed in the doeinge justice to such who expect the same &cr, and Further the Court Sees it of absolute Nesessity that A Court of Comissioners be called to meett the day before the Court of Tryalls setts at Warwicke: namely to asemble at Warwicke on the first Tuseday in November next to Tranceact such affayres as are of greate nesessity and concernment in the Collony: viztt Touchinge obstructions and Discoragements in trayneinge and what other matters may apeare urgant as writtinge to England Concerninge the letters received from the Unitted Collonies touchinge the people called Quakers &cr The Court is adjourned untill the First wedensday in Nor. next to be held at Warwicke.

At the Remeetinge of the Generall Court of Tryalls att Warwicke November the third: 1658

GRAND INQUEST

Captn John Cranston fore-man	John Easton
Thomas Greene	James Greene
John Richmond Senr	Obadiah Holmes
Joshua Coggeshall	Richard Carder
John Almy	Thomas Relph
Henry percy	John Lippitt senr

pettit jurry on

[M]r Greens case	[Th]omas Relph
[ob]diah Holmes foreman	[John] Lippitt senr
[Josh]ua Coggeshall	[John] Richmond senr
[Joh]n Easton	[Lott] strainge
[Rich]ard Carder	[George] Bliss

An action of the case of Trespas comenced by John Greene senr plaintiff against William Arnold Defendant Damidge 200 li: starll:

The Generall Ishue joyned by the Aturnies is not Guilty of the charge

The juries verdit we Finde for the plaintiff one hundred and fifty pownds Damage and the Cost of the Court: judgment graunted

The Defendant hath accordinge to law stopt the Exicution to have the case Reheard at the next Generall Court of Tryalls

Page 81

PETTITT JURRY

Captn John Cranston foreman	Richard Carder
obadiah Holmes	John Lippitt senr
Joshua Coggeshall	Caleb Carr

Thomas Relph	John Easton
Henry pearcy	John Richmond senr
Richard osbourne	James Ashton

An action of Debt by Bell Comenced by John Gerriardy plaintiff against Thomas Stanton

Defendant Damage 20 li

Ishue joyned by the Aturnies is not Guilty

Verditt wee Finde for the plaintiff seven pownds Damage and Cost of Court The Judgment Graunted

The Defendant hath accordinge to law stopt Exicution to have the case reheard at the next Generall Court of Tryalls

PETTITT JURRY ON THIS CASE

Captn John Cranston	Roger moory
obadiah Holmes	Ralph Earll senr
Joshua Coggeshall	Richard Carder
Thomas Relph	John Lippitt senr
Henry percy	James Ashton
Richard osbourne	Amoss Westcot

On A Reheareinge By the Defendant of the action of the Case For Trespas Comenced by Joseph Torry plaintiff against George Bliss Deffendant Damage twenty pownd The jurris Verdit we Finde for the Defendant Cost of Court: Judgment Graunted The plaintiff hath accordinge to law stopt the Exicution to have the case Reheard at the next Generall Court of Tryalls

An action of Debt upon the Case Comenced by Honorah Saull the wife of Thomas Saull of Flushin, plaintiff against John Cowdall of Newport Defendant Damage Sixty pownds The Defendant taken upon A Nihill Dicett The jurries Verdit we Finde for the plaintiff Damage thirty three pownds tenn shillings and Cost of Court. Judgement Graunted

Upon A presentment by the Generall Aturny against Anthony parrant for Atempting to procure an unlawfull asembly: the sayd parrant enters his Traverce pleads Guilty and refers him Selfe to the Judgement of the Bench: Whereupon the

Court doe order that the sayd Anthony parrant stands bownd in the Sum of tenn pownds starll to be of A peaceable and quiet Behavior towards all his highnes subjects untill the first of aprill next at which time the sayd parrant shall Repayre unto Mr William Baulston, and the Generall Recorder, and if nothinge in the meane time come in against him he shall then by them be cleared payinge Fees and that the Recorder shall record him at that time cleare of the afore-sayd Bond

Upon A presentment by the Generall Aturny Against Marie paull For Fornication her Father John Richmond senr, in her behalfe enters her Traverce: pleads Guilty and refers her to the judgment of the Bench. The Court doe judge her Guilty of Fornication and to be whipt or pay Forty Shillings according to law Judgment Graunted

Whereas Samuell Dyre and Mahorghalelheshbaz Dyre were bownd in A Bond of twenty pownds a peece to apeere at this instant Court, and they beinge called and not apeareinge the Court doe Declare their bonds to be Forfitt. Butt doe Defferr Exicution untill the First of Aprill next, and in the meanetime the Generall Treasurer to Demaund it of them before the next Court of Tryalls now insueinge, and that the Generall Treasurer if they refuse to pay it: is to acquaint them that the Court Deferred Exicution till the first of Aprill, that iff they apeere at the next Generall Court of Tryalls in march next at providence and there inform the Court the reason of their non apeareinge, and doe make Such Exscusis as may Satisfy the Court: the Court may medigate their Fines

Lawrance Wilkinson, Thomas Slow, and Thomas Clements chosen jurry-men for providence, they not atendinge the Court are fined tenn shillings a peece

Nathanill Browneinge is Fined tenn shillings, and Thomas Hazard five shillings

Page 82

The Genrl Courtt of Tryalls Held at providence the Second Tuseday in March beinge the 8th Day 1658-59

Mr Benidict Arnold presidtt
Mr William Feild Asistant
Mr Randall Howldon Asistant
Mr Richard Waterman } Deputies
Mr John Sayles } for providence
John Sanford Genrl Recod
Richard Knight Genrl Serjant
Mr John Greene Genrl Aturny

GRAND INQUEST

Mr Walter Todd foreman	Caleb Carr
Thomas Aingall	Toby: Saunders
James Ashton	James Greene
Thomas Olny junr	Vallintine Whitman
Hugh persions	John Richmond Senr
Mr John Gould off on A bill	William Carpenter
agst Tho Gould	Shedrec Manton

Thomas Roberts of providence beinge Desired by the Court to serve on the Grand Inquest and he Refusinge to serve useinge many improbrious and uncivill speeches to the Court sayinge that the Court were Fooles and he scorned to serve in such A way: Whereupon: The sayd Thomas Roberts stands Bownd to his highnes the lord protector of the Comon welth of England &cr, in the sum: of tenn pownds starll: to be of A peaceable and quiat behaviour towards all his highnes subjects dureinge this and the next Genrl Court of Tryalls to be held for the Collony the Second Tuseday in October next at portsmouth and then and there doe make his personall apeareance, or otherwise if the sayd Roberts shall come into this pressent Court and give satisfaction to the Court for his pressent misbehaviour then this bond is to be Voyde but otherwise to bee and stand in Force

It is ordered that the Genrl Treasurer shall pay out of the Treasury thirteene shills: to the grand inquest to provide them A Dinner Accordinge to law

PETTITT JURRY ON MR GREENS CASE

Walter Todd foreman	Toby Saunders
Thomas Aingall	Samuell Bennitt
James Ashton	Thomas Stafford
Thomas Olny junr	Shedrec Manton
Hugh persons	Edward Inman
John Gould	William White

Upon the Reheareinge of An Action of the Case of Trespas Comenced by John Greene plaintiff against William Arnold Defendt: Dam: 200 li starll:

The juries Verdict: Wee finde for the plaintiff wee give him Sixty pownds Damage and Cost of Courtt: judgment Graunted:

PETTITT JURRY ON JOSEPH TORRYS CASE

Walter Todd foreman	Toby Saunders
Thomas Aingall	Caleb Carr
James Ashton	Samuell Bennit
Thomas Olny junr	Thomas Stafford
Hugh persons	Shedrec Manton
John Gould	Edward Inman

Upon the Reheareinge of An Action of the Case for Trespas Comenced by Joseph Torry plaintiff against George Bliss Defendant Damage twenty pownds Starll: The jurris Verdict This is our Verdict Wee finde for the plaintiff wee give him fower pownds Damage and Cost of this Court all which is to be payd at peage Eight pr peny

Tatamoneshkish an Indian beinge Examained in Court sayth that he tooke out an Ancker of liquors out of William Cadmans cellar in the night time and that there was an other Indian with him Consentinge in the act whose name is Wonacomtone and that their habitation is at Cocomsquisitt near Mr Smyths Tradeinge howse

Quashawett an Indian sachim leiveinge at pocakett Doth beinde him Selfe his owne person to pay or caues to be payed & Delivered unto Captn Randall Houldon of Warwicke the full and just sum of Eight pownds twelve shillings to be payd at or before the next Genrl Court of Election to be held at providence to make Restitution to William Cadman for the loss of his liquors afore-sayd or else the sayd Sacham shall breinge and Deliver to the sayd Court of Election the afore-sayd Tatamoneshkish an Indian and the Sayd Quashawett doth binde him Selfe body for body for the sayd Indian: Tatamoneshkish. The Court doe Sentance the afore-sayd Tatamoneshkish an Indian to be whipt with fifteene stripes:

Thomas Gould beinge bownd to this Court and beinge Called in Court did not apeare Wherupon the Court did declare his bond to be Forfitt and if he doe not pay the General Treasurer the forfiture of his bond which is twenty pownd within tenn daies after the dessolution of this Court then Exicution is to goe forth against him provided he have notice thereof within six daies by the Genrl Treasurer

Jacob Mott beinge Bownd to this Court and beinge called in Court did not apeere wherfore the court doe declare his bond Forfitt and doe order Exicution to goe Forth, Except he shall within tenn daies after this court give bond to som: Genrl officer of this collony to answer what he was bownd to at the next Genrl Court of Tryalls to be held in october next at portsmouth, or else within the sayd tenn daies doe pay in the forfiture of his bond to the Genrl Treasurer, then the Exicution is to be stopt and Notice is to be given to him or to his Father by the Genrl Treasurer within six Dayes after the desolution of this Court.

Mary the wife of mathew Greenell beinge bownd and indicted for Fornication she enters her Traverce pleads guilty and refers her Selfe to the bench, Whereupon the Court doe adjudge her Guilty of Fornication and to pay Forty shillings or be whipt accordinge to law: judgment Graunted

Whereas Mr John Brigs was Bownd in a Bond of Fifteen pownds that Seweboion Alies Robin an Indian should macke his personal apeareance at this instant Court and the Sayd Indian apeareinge and atendinge the Court accordinge to bond,

the Courtt doe declare that the sayd Briges Bond is Fully performed and Null

William Dyre of Newport Senr Doth in this present Court
acknowlidge him Selfe indebted in the Sum of twenty pownds
starll to his highnes the lord protector of the Comon welth of
England &cr and that his Sones Samuell Dyre and Mehor-
shalelhasbaz Dyre shall macke their personal apeareances at
the next Genrl Court of Tryalls to be held at portsmouth, the
Second Tuseday in october next there to Answer to what
shall be aledged against them, whereupon the act of the last
Court of Tryalls is null & Exicution to be stopt and they
apeareinge this bond is voyd, but otherwise to stand in full
Force

Page 83

Whereas Quisuckquonch was by promise ingadged to apeare
at this Court and he not ape[aringe] It is ordered that the
Generall Aturny shall acquaint the sayd Quisuckquonch by
word [of] mouth or mesage that Either he send and pay the
remainder of the mony due to Rob[t] Griffin or Else apeare
at the next Court of election held in may next at providence
or Else there will be meanes ussed at that Court to Fetch him
in to macke Restitution.

Shedrech Manton Samuell Bennitt Edward Enman William
White and Thomas Stafford beinge putt on the jurry in the
abscence of som jurry-men, of portsmouth and Warwicke the
Sayd persons are ordered to have halfe their Fines from the
Genrl Treasurer as soone as it is Received by him, and it is
to be equaly devided amongst them.

Richard Sisson and William Cadman are fined each tenn
shillings apeece for not atending the jurry, mr John Smyth
& mr John Weekes are fined tenn shill: apeece for not atending the jurry, mr Fowler is Fined five shillings for not atendinge the jurry beinge putt on by the Court which five shills
shall be payd to Roger morry.

It is ordered that the Genrl Recorder shall give forth warrants From this Court to the shreiffe to Aprihend pumham for A Royall & Rescue, as also to aprehend those Indians offendinge in A Robbery done at pawtuxett: and that accordinge to the Generall Counsells order.

Upon a pettition of Richard pray the Court doe advise Richard pray to take by Authority the indian that hath wronged them in any Township in this Collony if he can be Fownd if not they may address themselves to the next Court of Commissioners for Redress in the matter.

The Court Desolved the 12th of march: 1658-9

Page 93

The Genrl Court of Tryalls Held for the Collony at portsmouth the 11th of October 1659

        Mr Benidict Arnold president
        Mr William Feild Asistant
        Mr William Baulston Asistant
        Mr Joseph Clarke Asistant
        Mr Randall Houldon Asistant
        Mr John Brigs   } Towne
        Mr John Roome   } Wardene
        John Sanford Genrl Recor
        Mr James Rogers Genrl Serjant
        Mr John Greene Genrl Aturny

GRAND JURRY-MEN

Mr John Gould foreman	Francis Brayton
Richard Sisson	Thomas Clarke
Richard pearce	Thomas Brooke
George Layton	James Greene
Thomas Brownell	Richard Carder
Thomas Kent	William Burton

Thomas Roberts apeareinge to Answer his Contempt at the last Court at Providence: the sayd Roberts doth in the Court acknowlidge his Fayleinge therein, as also Confesseth that it was his beinge distempered with drinke at that time that occasioned his then misbehaviour to the Court: Whereupon the Court doe order that the sayd Thomas Roberts payinge five shills for his beinge Distempered with drinke, to the Genrl Treasurer and pay officers Fees then he is cleared of his Former Bond

Anthony parrant Beinge bownd to this Court and also Indicted for breach of the peace by threats asault and battery, he apeareinge, confessed Guilty and Refers him Selfe to the judgment of the Bench, whereupon the Court doe acquit him of his bondes and the charge of indictmt payinge Fees

PETTITT JURRY ON THE STATS CASE AGST WILL DYRE

Mr John Gould foreman	John Greene
Richard pearce	Thomas Clarke
Georg Layton	Thomas Brooke
Thomas Brownell	James Greene
Frances Brayton	Richard Carder
Thomas Kent	William Burton

An action of the case for accompts and Debt concerninge the states parte of prices Comenced by the Genrl Aturny Mr John Greene in Behalfe of the Collony plaintiff against Nicholas Easton and William Dyre Defendts

The case demurd by the pla to the Genrl Court in march next, by vertue of the Genrl Court of Comissioners order only with Respect to Nicholas Easton, Ordered that the Tryall of the Case be Referred till tomorrow morneinge to See if possible the Genrl Treasurer and Genrl Aturny can Receive Satisfaction from William Dyre concerninge the accompt of the States parte which the Sayd Dyre Tenders in the Court, and if he doe not give them Satisfaction then the Case to proceed to Tryall.

The Genrl Ishue nott Guilty

On this Case the jurry haveinge beine longe upon it and they not agreeinge to any other but a spetiall verditt, The Court doe therefore by the Consent both of plaintiff and Defendant Will Dyre Referr the whole matter with Respect to

William Dyre as brought to this Court unto the next Court of Comissioners, And that the Sayd William Dyres Bonds doe stand good to ingadge him to answer the sayd matter at the Sayd Court of Comissioners

Upon an Indictment by the Genrl Aturny against Suckow an Indian For Fellony The Sayd Indian beinge brought into the Court and by the president Examined doth Confess that he did one time this Sumer Steale A Certaine percell of meals out of George Laytons Mill to the quantity of three fower or five pecks of meale, and he sayd that he did not Steale from thence at any other time

Whereupon the Court doe order that if the Sacham Wamsitta who accordinge to his Fathers Bond brought the aforesayd Indian to the Court, doe pay the sum of six pownd peage six pr peny unto the Generall Treasurer within Fowerteene daies from this time beinge the 13th day of October that then Wosomequins bond shall be delivered to Wamsitta But otherwise he shall Forfitt the sayd Bond, and to this order the sayd Wamsittas Counseler caled by the English Thomas an Indian in the Court did consent.

Upon two Indictments against Samuell Dyre and Mahorshalelhiashbash Dyre for Larceny against the state: Upon the Traverce they Confess Guilty and Referr them Selves to the Bench The Bench haveinge Duly Weighed the Matter of Fact charged against Samuell Dyre and Mahor Dyre doe finde and judge that it Falls under the Breach of the peace &cr And doe also finde that whereas the matter rose at first about Nontrayneinge and beinge also fuly informed and Convinced of their conformity unto order since the time of the promissed breach of peace, as also they both giveing good asureance in their Expressions of contineuinge in such conformity: the Court doe conclude that they have fuly satisfied the Law by their beinge Bownd Soe long, and by their peaceable behaviour and atendance at this Court, and doe hereupon Declare the fore-named Samuell and Mahor Dyre, are Quitt of their Bonds and charge and are Freed by proclamation paying Fees.

Upon an Indictment by the Genrl Aturny against Thomas Gould the sayd Thomas beinge called and he pleadeinge that he is not now Fitted for Traverce Desires the Court to Referr the Matter to the next court of Tryalls to be held at Newport: to which the Court doe Consent, he haveinge ingadged to the Court that his former Bond to the Court of Comissioners shall Continew in Force to breng him to Tryall at the next Court of Tryalls there to Answer the charge against him: And it is ordered that Sumons shall goe forth from the Recorder to Sumons him to the next Court at Newport.

George Layton foreman	Tho Clarke
Ral. Earll senr	Sam Sanford
Rich. perce	James Greene
Tho Brownell	Rich Carder
Fra Brayton	Danill Wilcock
Tho Kent	Will Burton

Upon an Indictment by the Genrl Aturny against Jacob Mott for Fornication, he beinge to apeare at this present Court, beinge called did not apeare Wherefore the Court doe Declare his Bond Forfitt

Upon An Indictment by the Grand Inquest against Richard Smyth for submittinge parts of the Collony to an other jurisdiction, he apeareinge in Court pleads he is not the man there charged and sayth he is not Richard Smyth of this Collony

juries Verditt Wee finde this Richard Smyth the man (Guilty) judgment Graunted

Whereas Robert Westcot was sumoned to this Court before he was in this Court indicted Therefore the Court doe order that Sumons shall goe forth from the Recor to Require the Sayd Robert Westcot to Answer indictment by the Genrl Aturny against him at the next Genrl Court of Tryals to be held at Newport

Page 94

. . . against Jacob Mott for Fornication the Court haveinge suff . . . latter end of the Court, provided he came and made his apeareance to answer to the charge before the Court was Ended: And he comminge and mackeinge his apeareance before the Court was fuly desolved, but not before the jurry was Dismissed, the Court Considered that he was com two late for A fayre Tryall [although he shewed his obediance in atendinge the Court] Seeinge the Court could not againe putt the jurry in A Legall capassity to goe on New Tryalls, they beinge Dismissed and dispersed. Yett the Court doth Conceive that his bond might have beine Remitted had it beine in their power Soe to Remitt, But Seeinge it was not the Court Doth Recomend the Consideration thereof to the next Court of Comissioners to Remitt the Sayd Fine hopeinge the Sayd Court will show him Favour therein: And withall the sayd Jacob Mott Stands Bownd in A Bond of tenn pownds to macke his personal apeareance at the next Genrl Court of Tryalls held at Newport in March next, and there to answer the charge Layd against him, And doe also order that Sumons presently goe Forth from the Recorder to Require the sayd Jacob Mott to Answer the Sayd indictment: Exicution is to be Suspended as touchinge the Bond above Forfitted untill the Court of Comissioners Result be given in that Matter

John Reed Beinge Bownd in A Bond of . . . pownds to apeare at this Court and he beinge called and not apeareinge the Court doe adjudg his bond Forfitt and Exicution accordinly to goe forth: Exicution given forth.

Edward Manton Henry Wright and John Feild chosen jurymen by the Towne of providence and they not atendinge that Service are fined each tenn shillings

The Genrl Court of Tryalls Held For the Collony Att Newport the 13th of March 1659 or ('60)

   Mr Benedict Arnold pressidt
   Mr William Feild Asistant
   Mr William Baulston Asistant
   Mr Joseph Clarke Asistant
   Capt Randall Houlden Asistant

Mr William Jeffery } Wardens
Mr Edward Smith   } for Newptt
John Sanford Genrl Recor
Mr James Rogers Genrl Serjant
Mr John Greene Genrl Aturny

Grand Jurry

Mr John porter Foreman	Thomas Stafford
Gerrard Bourne	John Richmond senr
Vallintine Whitman	Thomas Valston
Thomas Walwin	Henry Hobson
Caleb Carr	Bartholowmew Hunt
Joseph Torrey	Ralph Earl senr

An Action of the case for Accomptts and Debt concerneinge the states parte of prices Comenced by Mr John Greene Genrl Aturny in behalfe of the Collony pla against Mr Nicholas Easton Defendant Damage 400 li this case was twice Demurred once by Defendt & once by the pla The case beinge thre times Legaly caled in Court and the Defendt not apeareinge nor none for him to answer the Court doe declare the Bond Forfitt

An action of the case for Detayneinge Toby Knights Estate in Not Deliveringe the Sayd Estate and Refuseinge to give Security for it Comenced by Joseph Torrey Administrator by order and Authority of the Towne Counsell of Newport to the Estate of the afore-Sayd Toby Knight Deceased, plaintiff against John Coggeshall Defendant Damage 200 li str This case haveinge beine twice demurred once by defendendt and once by the plaintiff The Defendant beinge three times Legaly caled, and he not apeareinge nor any to answer for him the Court doe declare his bond Forfitt

Jurymen on Thomas Laytons Case

John Porter forman	Rich Tew
Vall Whitman	James Barker
Tho Walwin	John Randall

Adam Mott junr	Tho Stafford
Gerrard Bourne	Jer Willis
Ralph Earll senr	Fra Durbe

An action of the case Comenced by Thomas Layton plaintiff against John Richmond senr Damage 150 li starll: The juries Verdict Wee finde for the Defendant Cost of the Court judgment graunted

JURRYMEN ON CAPTN CRANSTONS CASE

John porter foreman	Rich Tew
Vall Whitman	Mr Tho Cooke
Tho Walwin	John Randall
Adam Mott junr	James Barker
Gerrard Bourne	Jer Willis
Caleb Carr	Fran. Durbee

An action of the case for Debt Comenced by Captn John Cranston plaintiff against Richard Knight Deffendant Damag 10 li starll: The Ishu joyned by the parties is not Guilty The jurris Verditt, Wee Finde for the plaintiff fower pownds tenn shills Debt, And thirty shills Damage at the rate of peage Eight pr penny and the Cost of the Court The Defendt haveinge given in duble bond and payd the bill of Cost hath A Reheareing graunted at the next Court of Tryalls

An action of the Case for Debt Comenced by John Sanford pla: against Nathanill Dickins Treasurer for the Towne of Newport and behalfe of the Sayd Towne Defendt Damag 10 li st This case was at the last court of Tryalls Demurred by the Defendt

The Defendt beinge twice Leagaly called thre times and he not apeareinge nor any to answer for him the Court doe declare his Bond Forfitt

An action of the Case For Debt upon accompt Comenced by Ralph Earll senr pla. against Richard Knight Defendt Damag: 10 li this case demurrd at the last Court by the defendt The Defendt beinge three times called in Court and not apeareinge nor any to answer for him the Court doe declare his Bond Forfitt

Page 95

An action of Trespas upon the Case Comenced by Ralph Earll Sen pla against [Richard Knight] Defendant Damag 20 li starll this case was demurrd by the Defendt the last Court The Defendant beinge three times caled and none apeareinge to answer the Courtt doe declare his Bond Forfitt

Whereas there is three action dependinge betweene Ralph Earll senr and Richard Knight two in this present Court and one Demurrd by the Defendt Earll, in the office, They doe both in the open Court Referr the sayd actions and all other Differences betweene them unto Mr Benidict Arnold president and Mr Randall Houldon Asistant to Ishu and Determin by award, and if they cannot agree on an award thereon, then Mr Edward Smyth is to be the Umpier, and if Mr Arnold and Mr Houldon cannot agree on an award then the sayd Umpier agreeinge with either of them shall Determine and Ishu the Sayd Differences and upon their agreement as afore-Sayd off an award then Exicution shall goe forth from the Recorder to Cause Either party to macke Restitution to the other accordinge to the sum the award shall mention as Authentickly as if the jurry had agreed on A verditt and the Court had graunted judgment thereon, and for performance thereof they in Court did Confess judgment Each to other

JURY MEN ON EDWARD BLUNTS CASE

Mr John porter foreman	James Barker
Vall Whitman	Captn Tho Cooke
Tho Walwin	John Randall
Gerrard Bourne	Tho Stafford
Caleb Carr	Jer Willis
Richard Tew	Fra Durbee

An action of the Case for Fraudilent Dealeinge and Breach of Covinant Comenced by Edward Blunt pla against Henry

Hobson Defendant Dam: 2oo li Starll: Taken pr nihill Dicett
The juries Verditt Wee finde for the plaintiff twenty two
pownds tenn shills Damage and the Cost of the Court Judgment graunted.

The Defendant haveinge accordinge to law putt in Duble
Bond and payd the bill of Cost hath A Reheareinge graunted
at the next Genrl Court of Tryalls in october next at Warwick

JURY-MEN ON WILLIAM FEILD &CR CASE

Mr John porter foreman	James Barker
Vall Whittman	Captn Tho Cooke
Tho Walwin	Adam Mott junr
Gerrard Bourne	John Randal
Caleb Carr	Wm Weden
Rich Tew	Jer Willis

An action of Trespas upon the case Comenced by William
Feild William Harris Zachery Roades and William Carpenter
plaintiffs against Mr John Smyth Treasurer for the towne of
Warwick and in the sayd Townes behalfe Defendant Damag
1oo li starll

The Ishue joyned by the Aturnies is Genrl (Not guilty)
The juries Verditt Wee finde for the plaintiffs two pence
Damag and Cost of the Court judgment graunted

JURY MEN ON RICHARD KNIGHTS CASE

Mr John porter foreman	Ralph Earll senr
Vall Whitman	Adam Mott junr
Tho Walwin	Christop: Haukshurst
Gerrard Bourne	Ralph Earll junr
Captn Tho Cooke	William Harris
John Randall	Tho Harris junr

An action of the Case for Debt by Genrl Court order
Comenced by Richard Knight plaintiff against Nathanill
Dickins Treasurer for the Towne of Newport and in behalfe
of the Sayd Towne Defendt: The Ishu joyned is not guilty

The jurys Verditt wee finde for the Defendt the Cost of the Court

The Court doe unanimously agree that the verditt brought in by the jurry in the Case of Richard Knight against Nathanill Dickins afore-Sayd, the Sayd Verditt is Contrary to law and therefore Suspend Judgment thereon.

An action of the case for Trespas Comenced by peeter Taelman plaintiff against Adam Mott senr Defendant Damag 30 li starll: The Ishu joyned by the Aturnie (Not Guilty)

Whereas the Jurry have beine long on the Case between Mr Taelman and Adam Mott senr and three times sent forth by the Court thereon, And the jurry Declareinge that they cannot agree on A Verditt on the Sayd case: Therefore both the plaintiff and Defendant have in the Court agreed to Referr the Matter in Difference unto Mr Benedict Arnold president and to Mr Randall Houldon Asistant and if they cannot agree then Mr Edward Smyth is to be the umpier thereon, and what and what the Sayd Mr Arnold and Mr Houldon shall agree and award on, or else either of them with Sayd umpier, the Sayd parties plaintiff and defendant doe in the Court acknowlidg Judgment Each to other, to performe their award And if Either party shall neglect to performe the award: Then Exicution to goe forth as legaly upon the award, as if the jurry had agreed upon A verditt on the Sayd case and the Court graunted jugment thereon.

Upon A petition to this court from Mr William Arnold of pawtuxett Dated the 26th of the 12th month Desireinge justice against the Indians that Voyolenly tooke away his goods the last yeare &cr The Court doe order the Genrl Recor in their behalfe to signify to Mr Arnold that there shall be a serious course taken for his releife, and Desire him in meane time to be patient in the Exspectation thereof in all convenient Sort as also to Signify that the Case of warwick is som what of licke nature and they also patiently yett Earnistly doe Exspect justice speedily:

Jurymen on tho Goulds and Jacob Motts Cases.

Mr John porter f. m:	James Barker
Vall Whitman	Jno Richmond Senr
Tho Walwin	Jer Willis
Gerrard Bourne	Tho Stafford
Caleb Carr	Ralph Earll senr
Rich Tew	Fra Durbee

An Indictment by the Genrl Aturny against Thomas Gould for Breach of the peace by Ausault and Battery

Enters his Traverc and beinge demaunded Whither Guilty or not guilty pleads he knowes he is not Guilty: The juries Verditt Wee finde Thomas Gould Guilty of the Breach of the peace tenn shillings Damag and Cost of the Court judgment graunted, haveinge payd the fine and charges he the Sayd Gould is acquitted in Court by proclamation.

Upon an Indictment by the Genrl Aturny against Jacob Mott for Fornication: he Enters his Traverce and pleads Not Guilty: The jurris Verditt Wee finde for the Defendt Not Guilty the sayd Jacob Mott haveinge payd his Fees is cleered in Court by proclamation

The presentments against Richard Smith Captn Hutchinson Leiutn Hudson as also against Leiutn Robert Westcot for breach of the law that is against purchasinge of lands in the Collony from the Indians without order from A Court of Comissioners &cr are for present Suspended from beinge further prossicuted at this present Court for Severall Reasons that are with the Court Weighty on that behalfe: And therefore Desire the law-makeinge Asembly may have the further scaninge of it before further proceeds be made therein by this Court.

Upon an Indictment by the Genrl Aturny against Mary Reed for Fornication, upon the Traverc beinge Demaunded whither Guilty or not She owned Guilty The Court doe suspend judgment till the next Court of Tryalls in october next at Warwick, and in the meane time her bonds to continew in force to breinge her to that Court

JURRY MEN ON NATH: WATERMANS CASE

Mr. John porter foreman	Jerrith Bull
Joshua Coggeshall	John Richmond Senr
Gerrard Bourne	Jer Willis
Caleb Carr	Thomas Stafford
Rich Tew	Ralph Earll Senr
Hen Bull	Christo Haukshurst

Upon an Indictment by the Genrl Aturny against Nathaniell Waterman for Fornication, enters his Traverce pleads not Guilty. The juries Verditt (Not Guilty) haveinge payd his Fees he is cleared by proclamation in Court,

The Court doe acquitt Jacob Mott from his Forfiture at the last Court and from his bond at the last Court of Tryalls wherein he was bound to apeare at the next Court of Comissioners

postcript

Page 96 . . . doe unanimosly agree to suspend Exicution untill the Court of Comissioners in may next be ended in all those cases wherein the Defendants have forfitted their Bonds by nonapeareance and after the sayd Court of Comissioners is Ended Exicutions goe forth

Edward Enman chosen A jurry man for providence is fined tenn shillings where of five shills is offsett for 5 s due to him for Serveinge on the jury at providence

Robert Hazard chosen A jurry-man by portsmouth, is fined tenn shills

Thomas Bradly for not serveinge on the jurry beinge chosen by warwick is fined tenn shills as also Mathias Harvie fined tenn shills of which 10 s: Francis Durbe is to have Five shills

Finnis

Page 98

The Generall Court of Tryalls Held for the Collony at Warwick the 9th of october: 1660

Grand Inquest
Foreman Mr peeter Taelman

John Fenner	James Greene
phillip Tabor	Thomas Hopkins
Caleb Carr	John Richmond Senr
Thomas Gould	John Richmond junr
John Greene	Thomas Harris junr
Richard Carder	

Mr William Brenton president
Mr William Feild Asistant
Mr William Baulston Asistant
Mr Benedict Arnold Asistant
Mr John Greene Asistant
Mr John Smyth }
Mr Walter Todd } Wardens for Warwick
John Sanford Genrl Recor
James Rogers Genrl serjant
Mr John Easton Genrl Aturney

Jurymen on the states case

phillip Tabor foreman	Caleb Carr
John Fenner	Tho Gould
peeter Taelman	John Greene
Daniell Browne	Henry Hobson
John Richmond senr	James Greene
Thomas Hopkins	Richard Carder

An action of the Case for Accompts and Debt Concerneinge the States parte of prices Comenced by Mr John
Greene Genrl Aturney in behalfe of the Collony plaintif
against Mr Nicholas Easton defendt
Damage:
The Ishue joyned by the Aturnies is not Guilty:
Whereas the jurry have beine three daies on the action
betweene the state and Mr Easton, and they comeinge into
the Court declared that they could not agree on A verdict,
Therefore both plaintiff and defendant doe Consent in this
present Court to Refer the Case to the next Genrl Court of

Tryalls to be held the second Tuseday in march next at providence, and that the defendants bonds doe still stand in force to breing him to A Leagall Tryall at the Sayd Court by his free Consent in this Court.
Jurymen on Blunts Case

Richard Townsend foreman	Thomas Hopkins
philip Tabor	Caleb Carr
John Fenner	Thomas Gould
Thomas Relph	John Greene
Daniell Browne	James Sweet
John Richmond senr	Richard Carder

Upon the Reheareinge of An action of the Case for Fraudilent dealing and Breach of Covinant damage 200 li: starll: Comenced by Edward Blunt plaintiff against Henry Hobson Defendant

The Ishue Joyned by the Aturnies is not Guilty

The Juries Verdict wee finde for the plaintiff Twenty two pounds and Cost of Court Judgment graunted and Exicution thereon.

Juriemen on William Harris &cr their Case
philip Tabor foreman

Richard Townsend	Thomas Hopkins
John Richmond senr	Captn Richard Morris
John Fenner	peeter Taelman
Daniell Browne	Henry Hobson
Thomas Gould	John Richmond junr
John Greene	

Upon the Reheareing of an action of Trespas upon the Case Comenced by William Feild William Harris Zachery Roades and William Carpenter Plaintiffs against John Smyth Treasurer for the Towne of warwick and in the sayd Townes Behalfe Defendant Damag 100 li starll:

The Jurries verdict Wee finde for the defendant Damag fower pence and cost of Court Not medling with title of Land: judgment graunted

The plaintiffs haveing performed the law in that case provided have Liberty of A Reheareing the next Court of Tryalls to be held the second Tuseday in march next at providence

Jurymen on Mr Gortons case

Richard Townsend foreman	Tho Hopkins
Philip Tabor	Caleb Carr
John Fenner	Thomas Gould
Daniell Browne	John Greene
Thomas Relph	Richard Carder
John Richmond senr	James Greene

An action of Trespas upon the Case for unjust Detaynure Comenced by Samuell Gorton Senr plaintiff against Zachary Roades Defendant Damag Starll

The Ishue Joyned is not Guilty of the charge

The Juries Verdict Wee finde for the Defendant two pence Damage and Cost of Court

Judgment graunted

Jurymen on Gerriardys case

Joseph Torrey foreman	Caleb Carr
Philip Tabor	Thomas Hopkins
John Fenner	John Greene
Daniell Browne	peeter Taelman
Thomas Relph	James Greene
John Richmond Senr	Henry Hobson

Upon an apeale of an action of the Case Concerneinge Accompts and Debt Comenced by John Gerriardy plaintiff against Robert Westcott Defendant Damag starll which sayd action was Comenced in Warwicke Towne Court

The Ishue Not Guilty: The Juries Verdict Wee finde for the Defendant two pence damag Cost of this Court Judgment Graunted And the plaintiff haveing performed the Law in that Case provided hath his Libertie to have his Case Reheard in the next Genrl Court of Tryalls to be held in providence

it beinge also by this Courts aprobation which is viztt:

The Court doe Judge it Lawfull and therefore order that
John Gerriardy shall if he see cause have A Reheareing
performeing the Law in that case provided

Mary Read being Caled in Court and not apeareing when
Caled Therefore the Court doe order that her bonds doe still
continew in force to breing her to the next Court to be held
in March next at providence

The Court order that the Indians

Page 100

The Genrl Court of Tryalls Held for the Collony at
providence the 12th of march 1660 or (61)
  Mr. William Brenton president
  Mr William Feild Asistant
   Mr Benedict Arnold Asistant
  Mr John Greene Asistant
  Mr William Carpenter⎰
  Mr Thomas Olney   ⎱ Wardens for providence
  John Sanford Genrl Recor
  James Rogers Genrl Serjant
  Mr John Easton Genrl Aturney

GRAND INQUEST

Mr Thomas Harris foreman	Thomas Harris junr
Thomas Arnold	Lawrance Turner
Thomas Roberts	William Burton
John Richmond Senr	John Sweete
Roger Morie	John Smyth
John Fenner	Edward Larkin

Benjamin Hernden is by order of the Court Comitted to
the Serjants Custody till be be Tryed Whereas there is a
Case that depended between, Mr John Greene Genrl Aturny
in the Collony behalfe plaintiff and Nicholas Easton Defendant, about the States parte of prizes &cr: the Court at
this time haveing Seariously weighed the matter: as also Red

and Considered the Collonyes order made for Demaund of the sayd Estate, doe conceive that it is not Conveniant to prosicute the sayd Action any further untill that Court of Comissioners of this Collony doe take further order for the mannagment of the matter in Regard that there are very greate alterations &cr. since the former order was made: And therefore the Court doe unanimosly agree in Referring the matter to the next Court of Comissioners as afore-sayd Whereas a case depending between Mr William Feild of providence &cr against Mr John Smyth Treasurer of War- wick, is called, But that there being not a legall Jurry to be had for the Tryall of it, The Court upon Necessitie are forced to wave it for present till the next Court to be Tryed, and then to proceed where a Jurry may be had that is in law capable, and both plaintiff and Defendant doe agree to and stand bownd then and there to prosicute and answer, and although William Carpenter one of the plaintiffs doth not prosicute yett the defendant is content at the next Court to answer the other three: And their bonds to continew to the sayd Court of Tryalls to be held at portsmouth in October next

Jno Gerriards Case

PETTITT JURREY

Arthur Fenner foreman	Thomas Arnold
John Browne	Benj. Smyth
Jerrith Bull	John Richmond Senr
Edward Larkin	Christ. Haukshurst
Lawrance Turner	Tho Hopkins
Henry Ruddick	Thomas Harris

Upon the Reheareing of an action concerneing accompts and Debt Comenced by John Gerriardy plaintiff against Robert Westcott Defendant and Tryed the Last Court of Tryalls:

Jurries Verdict Wee finde for the Defendant Judgment Graunted

Upon an Indictment by Genrl Aturny against Waumaion

an Indian for murthering John Clawson of the Towne of providence on the Forth daie of January in the Evening in the yeare 1660 (61) The sayd Indian being Called and asked by Interpreters in this Court whither he had killed the sayd Clawson or not, he Confessed that he had killed him. The Court have agreed to pass Centance against the sayd Indian The Court doe order the Genrl Recorder to give forth order and Comission to the Genrl Serjant or shreife Forthwith to Exicute the Indian Waumaion and hang him till he be dead dead

Herndens Case

PETTITT JURRY

Arthur Fenner foreman	John Browne
Henry Ruddick	Benj Smyth
peeter Easton	John Sayles
Thomas Hopkins	peeter Taelman
Stephen Arnold	Richard Townsend
Zachery Roades	Edward Smyth

Upon an Indictment by the Genrl Aturney against Benjamin Hernden of the Towne of providence for Suspition of being A princeple in Murther Comitted by Waumaion an Indian upon John Clawson The sayd Benjamin Hernden being Called and asked wither Guilty or Not Guilty: pleads not Guilty and Refers him Selfe for Tryall to god and the Cuntrey.

The Jurris Verdict Wee find Benjamin Hernden Not Guilty) he is cleered by proclamation in this present Court paying Fees.

Marie Reade being bownd to this Court is by the Court acquitted paying fees

Upon Indictment against Cagontoossuck an Indian for Robbery &cr Done against James Greene John Lippitt senr, and William Burton all of Warwicke: The fore-sayd Indian being Called: the Shreife made answer that the Sayd Indian had made an Escape, and Soe was not here to answer But the persons afore named being Caled to prosicute did make

their lawfull apeareance according as they were bownd.
Ordered by the Court that Woutous have his Fetters taken
off being him Selfe and his brother Wotoxsha have ingadged
to his majtie body for body for their lawfull apeareance at
the next Genrl Court of Tryalls to be holden at portsmouth
their to Answer the Complaynt of Mr William Arnold of
pawtuxett Furthermore, Mr William Arnold aforesayd doth
Ingadge in the Court that he will be there to prosicute
Woutous afore-Sayd by him Selfe or his Aturny
Mr William Almy Mr Richard Burdin phillip Sheareman
Edward Fisher and Thomas Layton chosen Jurry-men by
the Towne of portsmouth, they not atending the Court are
fined tenn shillings a peece
Mr. John Gould and Mr. John Coggeshall chosen Jurry-men
by the Towne of Newport they not atendinge the Court are
fined tenn shillings a peece

Page 106

The Gennerall Court of Trialls held at portsmouth October
the: 8: 1661

>   Mr William Brenton presedent
>   Mr William Feeld asistante
>   Mr William Baulston Asistante
>   Mr Bennedicke Arnall Asistante
>   Mr John Greene Asistante
>   Mr John Roome ⎱
>   Mr John Breedge⎰ Wardens
>   Joseph Torrey Recorder
>   Mr James Rogers Gen Sargante
>   Mr John Easton gen Atornie

GRANJURY

Mr John porter forman	Mr William Harris
Mr William Almie	Mr Thomas Layton
Mr James Badcocke	Mr Thomas Clarke

Mr Richard Dun   Mr Samuell Wilbore
Mr Frances brayton   Barthelmew Hunt
Mr Steven Arnolt   Mr John Gariardie

The presentment of the Grand Jury
We the Grand Jury doe Indite Robert Westcote of Warwicke for breach of peace in Stricking Mr John Greene of Warwicke Gennerall Asistante Contrary to the peace of the kings Crowne and Dignitie Wee the Grand Jury doe Indict James Woodward of portsmouth and Mary Hick wife of Gabriel Hick that Contrary to law they weare found in bead Together

A reheareing of an action of Trespas upon the Case Commenced by Mr William Feeld, William Harris Zachery Roads and William Carpender plaintiffs against Mr John Smith Tresurer for the towne of Warwick and in the behalfe of the towne of Warwick defendant damedge 100 pound Starlinge

Jurymen on Will Harris

John Smith   Captain Hopson
Frances Brayton   Thomas Layton
James Badcocke   Thomas Clarke
Richard Dun   Batholomew Hunt
Hugh Persons   Peledg Shearman
Edward Larken   Richard Bulger
Henry Hobson

And for as much as ther apeares some obstroction in the proceeds in that action dependinge betwixt the aforenamed Mr Feeld William Harres Zachery Roades and William Carpender plaintive against Mr John Smith Tresurer of the towne of Warwicke: becaues there is not a letter of atornie that doth oltharrize William Harris to proceed as formerly and that it doth also apeare that William Carpender did desarte the cause: therefore to tacke of al scruples that may arise by the Defendant Mr William Feeld and William Harres doth ingage in open Court them Selves in a bond of five hundred pounds that they will macke good the

Damedge that shall arise upon the Isue of this Sute and Stand to the verdett and Judgment of this Court in the Case

The verdite of the jurry is, Wee finde for the Defendante with ther Chardes and Cost of the Courte: Judgment granted by the Courte

September 10: 1660

JURRYMEN IN THOMAS LAYTONS CASE

Captayne Hopson	Larkin
Francis Brayton	Richard Bulger
James Badcocke	Henry Hobson
Thomas Clarke	Geriardy
Richard Dun	Thomas Bronell
Parsons	William Almie

An Action entred by Thomas Layton against John Richman Senr for   Damadg
300 pound the Issue is not Guilty

The verdict is wee finde for the playntive Cost of the Court Judgment Granted by the Court

An Action Commensed by Mr Benedicke arnall against Cocaunaguant Sachim of the narragansett for Dbte damadge 25 pound (the verdict of the Jury) is wee finde for the plaintife five pound padge at Sixe pr peine and the little or five pound wompome Sixe pr penie Cost of the Courte and two penie Damadge Judgment Granted by the Courte

JURY ONE BOTH ———— CASES IS

captayne Hopson forman	Richard Bulger
Francis Brayton	Hennery Hobson
John Porter	John Gaarrardie
James Barker	William Almie
Richard Dun	Thomas Clarke
Edward Larkin	Barthelmew Hunt

THE JURY ONE ROBT WESCOTE

Present was Captyn Hobson

Francis Brayton	Thomas Bronell
John Porter	Tho Layton

James Barker
Richard Dun
Edward Larkin
Richard Bulger

Hennery Hobson
Thomas Clarke
Barthelmew Hunt

An action Commenced by Mr Randall Holden against moeallicke an Indian of dbte upon the Case damedge fiftie pound Starlinge (The verdict of the Jurie is) wee finde for the plaintife twenty Eight pound Seventen Shillings and five pence dbte Wompon Sixe a penie Damedge five pound and Cost of the Court Judgment Granted by the Court

October the 18:1660 Mr John Easton Generall atornie Commenceth a Sute against Mr Samuell Gorton Senr of warwick for Slander of the Court this Case was demured by the playntive at the Court held at portsmouth October the 7:1661

Concearning the action that was Commenced by Mr John Easton Against Mr Samuell Gorton of Warwicke and the playntife not apearinge in Court to prosicute and the Defendante pleading and tendering ther answer theare acording to the libertie of law, none beinge there to prosicute the Sute the Court doe declare that the action fales

Robert Westcote being Indicted by the grand Jury for breach of peace in Sriking Mr John Greene of warwicke generall asistant Contrary to the peace of the kings Crowne and dignity put him Selfe upon the travice and pleads not Guilty (the verdite of the Jury)

Wee finde for the kings maieste fortye shillings fine and Cost of the Court

Judgment granted by the Court

At the Generall Court held at portsmouth the 11 of october 1661 James Woodword and Mary Hicke the wife of Gabriel Hicke both of portsmouth was presented by the Grand Jury for being in Bead together Contrary to law — but in respecte the law provids that ther shall be two wittneses for the profe of the facte: and ther beinge but one wittnes and hee under age yett the forsd parties: out of the Conviction of ther Consciences did freely Confese the ofence and Did Desier the favore of the Court and the Court finding that ther was no person —— Could any be prevayled with : that would Convict the Sayd persons and noe witnes Did apeare to prove that James Woodword had a wife then living the Court Resoulve that James Woodword shall pay forty shillings and in regard Mary Hicke wife to Gabriel Hicke was —— by reson that she hath latly layen in) Shee is by the Courte order reprieved from heear sentence untill the next Court of Triales heald at nuport the Second Tusday of march next her husband standing bound for her apearance in a bond tenn pound

John Fenner and Daniell Browne Chosen Jury men for the towne of providence and not apearing are finid ten shillings apiece by the Court and to pay it acording to the law Hennery bull and Jerimiah Willes chosen jurie man for the towne of nuport and not apearing are fined ten shillinges apeece by the Courte and to pay it according to the law

Page 107

Mathias harvie of the towne of Warwick was Chosen Jurie man for the towne and not apearing was fined ten shillinges by the Court and to pay it according to law

It is ordered by the Court that the recorder shall Suplie the gennerall atornies place in the absence of the gennerall atornie in the Case betwixt His Maieste and Robert Westcote it is ordered that the recorder shall give forth prosses to the Gen Sargant to Destrayne or tocke—the fines of the Jurie men that did not apeare and weare fined by the Court which is John fenner Daniell Browne Hennery bull Jeremiah Willes Mathias harvi: John Sweett

The proceeds of a Courte of Triall held at

Nuport march 11 :1661 or 62

    Mr William Brenton presedente

    Mr William feild asistant for providence

    Mr William Baulston asistant for portsmouth

    Mr Benedect Arnall asistant for nuport

Mr John Greene asistant for warwick
Mr John Easton warden for nuport
Mr Richard Tew debete warden
Joseph Torrey recorder
Mr James Rogers Gennerall Sargant
Mr Caleb Carr Gen Tresurer
Mr John Easton Gennerall Atornie

Grand Jury

Mr William Dyer forman

John Alsborow

Thomas Crowell

Edward fissher

John peperde

John Wood

John Crendall

Mr Walter Tood

Mr Edmon Calverly

Tobias Sanders

hennery Temberlidge

John Cowdall

March 11 : 12th 1661-62

Wee The Juriours for the Soveraigne Lord the king doe presente John Easton and Richard Tew wardens of the towne of nuport for not repairinge the Stocks and keepinge them in due order as also that they have not Caused A whippinge poste to be sette up in the saide towne: both which beinge defecttive is Contrary to the peace Crowne and Dignity of his maieste

Wee The Juriouess for, or Soueraigne Lord the king doe presente Robert Westcote of warwicke who did upon the 26th of february last past Enter into the house of water todd of warwick aforesd in or about the tenth hour of the night and did thear and then from the sd water feloniously tacke and beare away an estate to the valew of five hundred pound starling which is Contrary to the peace Crowne and Dignity of his maiestie

Wee the Juriouers for or soveraigne lord the king doe present the towne of warwicke for Default of stockes and whipping post being Contrary to the peace Crowne and dignity of the maieste

An action of the Case for Debte Entered by henry hobson against Ralph Earll Junr Damedge twenty pound

The Gennarall Issue Joyned by the atornies not gylty
The verdite we find for the plaintive the horse bargained
for Damedge three pounds fifteene shillings in marchantable
stronge peege and Cost of Courte.

JUDGMENTE GRANTED

Jurymen in the Case betwixt henry hobson and Ralph Earll
Ju

John porter	John peperde
frances brayton	John Wood
John trep	Thomas valstone
William Devell	Barthellmue west
James Man	John Almie
John Crandall	Thomas brownell

Mary hicke beinge Called beinge bound to apeare at this
Courte not apearing Gabrell hicke beinge bound in a bond of
10 pound for his wife maryes apearance and not apearinge
beinge Called the Courte doe Judge the the bond to be forfitted
  The Jury upon the Case betwixt the King and Robert
Westcote

John porter	John Crandall
frances brayton	John peperde
John trep	John wood
William Devell	Thomas valstone
James man	barthelmue west
William Letherland	Edward Smith

Robert Westcote beinge presented by the Grand Jury for
that hee ded upon the [26th] of february Last past Enter
into the howse of walter Tod of warwicke and did about
the tenth hour of the night beare away an Estate to the
value of five hundred pound Starlinge feloneously beinge
Called Denies the Charge and puts himself upon the triall
  Ther beinge A presentemente brought against Robert
Westcote and hee beinge bound by the Court for felonyous
tacking away an Estate Robert Westcote beinge Called in
& pleades not gylty and puts himselfe upon the triall and the

Gennerall atorney beinge absente whose place it is to plead such matters as Consearnes the kings maieste whereupon the Courte doe Request and apoynt the Recorder to saple the atorneys pl[ace] in the Case betwixt the kings maieste and Robert Westcote one his maiestie behalfe

The verdit of the Jury one the Case betwext the king and Robert Westcote
We find the presonor at the bar not gylty of felonye in tackinge away the   .   .   .

Judgment Granted the presoner to be free
paying fees

INDEX

VIII

RHODE ISLAND COURT RECORDS

- 1662-1670 -

Volume #2

Records
of
The Court *of* Trials
of
The Colony
of
Providence Plantations

Southern Historical Press, Inc.
Greenville, South Carolina
PROVIDENCE
1922

PUBLICATION COMMITTEE

HENRY D. SHARPE
GEORGE L. SHEPLEY
NORMAN M. ISHAM

The present publication of the Rhode Island
Historical Society continues the reprinting of the
Court Records, which was begun in the preced-
ing volume of the same title.

RHODE ISLAND COURT RECORDS

Page 116

The proceed of a Court of Trialls held at warwicke october
14 1662
Mr. Benedict Arnall presedent
Mr. William Field Asistant
Mr. William Baulstone Asistant
Mr. Richard Tew Asistant
Mr. John greene Asistant
Mr John Smith warden for the towne of warwicke
Mr John Weckes Asistant
Joseph Torrey Recorder
Mr James Rogers gen Sargent
Mr John Sanford gen Atornye

GRAND JURYMEN

Mr John gould foreman
Mr. John Bridges
Mr James Badcocke
Mr George Gardener
Mr Samuell Wilbore
Mr John Tripp

Mr Thomas Brownelle
Mr frances Brayton
Mr Caleb Carr
Mr Mathias Harvie
Mr Thomas Greene
Mr James Greene

THE JURY

Mr John gould
frances brayton
george gardenner
Caleb Carr
Samuel Wilbore
John Tripp

John Swett
James Swett
Thomas Relph
Richard Carder
John Leppitt
James badcocke

An action Entered by Mr Randall howldon against James
Rogers Shrife and gennarall Sargant Dammadge 80 pound.

Whereas in the Case Depending betwixt Mr Randall Howlden plaintiffe and James Rogers gennerall Sargent Defendant : the plaintiffe pleads ther is noe answer put In by the Defendante in the sayd Case: and therfore Craves a nihill disitt to be alowed the Court doe declare that the law is Cleare that a nihill disitt be taken : and yett the Defendant hath Liberty to put In his answer in the Court in this Case being present and Requier the benifitt of the law :

 The answer being put In the Case goes to the Jury

Ther being a bill presented by the atorny gennerall aganst John Smith living at Cononicott for specking words of reproch aganst Mr Binidick Arnold presedent which words did absolutly tend to his disparedgment in the Excicution of his office the sayd Smith being bound to this Court and being Called Confeseth himselfe guilty and Referes himselfe to the beench.

The sentance of the Court is

Whereas John Smyth Inhabiting within this Collony Dwilling at presant upon Quononicott Iland being bound to this Court and heare Indicted by the Atorny gennerall for useing words of reproch aganst the presedent Mr. Benedict Arnold in the Excicution of his office : and the Bill of Indictment found by the Grand Jury : the Sayd John Smyth being Called to answer to the Charge : Confeseth himselfe Guilty of the Sayd Charge and Sayth hee hath malisiously Rashly and without grownds Reproched the presedent in saying that hee gave out warrant to aprehend the wife of william Ayres who was sent after from Quoneticott for breacking prison : and that having given out his warrant Did send private notice to the Sayd Smiths howse that the woman might be Convayed away soe to Escape the sayd warrant : as also in useing many other speeches of Contempt touching the presedent and government in A Reprochful maner and the Sayd John Smith Doth Submitt himselfe to the Court desiering ther favour : not to Inflict upon him the Extremity of Rigour for his Sayd offense.

Whereupon the Court Respectinge the peace and safty of the Kings Subiects : and In order therto the honour of the govern-

ment Excercised under his maiestye in this Collony and not the
Destroying but the Reforming of such as are in Legall sort
Reformable doe therfore bind the Sayd John Smith unto his
good behavour untill the next gennerall Court of trialls in a
bond twentye pound and In Case hee accordingly behave himselfe peacably and submisively to his maiestyes Subiects : and
government in this Collony and alsoe provided the Sayd John
Smith doe sett up with his one hand A Coppie of this his
acknowlidgment written and fasten it upon the post of the
Doore at the Entrance of the prison porch at nuport at the
Command and In the presance of the generall Sargant and
whome he Shall apoynt to see it Done : and upon the performance of the whole Ingagement his bonds to be voyd : otherwise
to stand in full force and vertue.

Whereas Margrett the wife of John Smyth of Quononicott
is bound to apeare at this Court and hath petitioned the Court
for weightty Resones declared therin to Excuse her not apearing
now, but to acquit her or to order her to apeare at next gennerall Court & : the Court doe declare that John Smith afore-
sayd doe Ingage to the Court in A bond of twentye pound for
his wife her appearance at the Sayd Court accordingly which
Court is alsoe in his maiesties name to be holden at providence
the Second Tueday in march next : that Shee then and there
answer to what She hath bene Engageed to Concerning her
Charge aganst georg gardenner of nuport Junior

Page 117

The Jury one georg gardenner Junior

William harris	Samuell Wilbore
James Badcocke	frances Brayton
John Tripp	Richard osborne
henry knowles	Thomas olnye
John Bridgs	andrew harris
James greene	francis usselton

Ther being a bill pesented by the atorny gennerall aganst
George gardenner Juniour of nuport for useing and specking

words of Contempt and Reproch aganst Mr Benidick Arnold presedent in the Excicution of his office which word weare spocken about the 10 of July last the sayd georg gardenner being bound to the Court and being Called and Alsoe what hee Sayd to the bill of Indictment whether guilty or not guilty he pleads not guilty and traverset the bill

the verditt of the Jury is
we find Not guilty

The Jury

Richard Carder	John garriardy
John Swett	Joseph Carpender
James Swett	amos Westcott
Thomas harris Jun	John potter
vallinton whitman	Jerimiah Westcott
Thomas bradly	Thomas Stafford

Ther being A bill present by John hodson aganst petter Tollman for a Chetter in Chetting Ann Elton and her Children of Three hundred pound in the third yeare of the Rayne of Charles the Second king of England Scotland france and Ireland and the Dominioe therto belonging.

the Sayd Tollman being present Traverath his Indictment pled not guilty

(The verdict of the Jury) wee find not guilty Ther being matter presented to the Court by John hodson now prisnor under the Costoudye of James Rogers gennerall Sargant (in poynt of action) and the sayd hodson being in the Collony A non Resedent the Court Requiering security of him for any matter that hee may Ingage In : hee doth freely yeld and give up himselfe A prisonor to Remayne in the hands of the Sayd James Rogers gennerall Sargant or any other that may Succeed him in that place untill all matters be Ended that hee shall put on foot by Indictment now began in this Court be Ended

To the president and gennerall Court of Trialls held for the Collony of providince plantationes Begun at warwicke october 14th : 1662

Wheras I John hodson have Indicted petter Tollman at this Court for A Chetter and the bill found by the grand Jury hee

hath traversed his Indictment and pleaded not guilty and therupon the Triall is with the petty Jury &c and for ther Remem-
bering how much this Collony hath beine Excercised with the
hearing of the Differances Relating to petter Tollman Ann
Elton and my selfe &c : both formerly and lattely to the great
Distorbance of the Inhabitance by Reson of the.......... of
the matters in Controverccy amongst the persones before
named : I the Sayd John hodson growing senseable of the
further Troble that may yett Insue to the Collony therby : and
being Realy afected therwith and Desirouse to Save the honuar
and peace of the Collony : doe therfore before the petty Jury
doe bringe in ther verdict Desier the Court to grant mee an
apeale to the king's bench in England whear I may procicutte
the matters in Controvercy : and upon the grant hearof sha[ll]
Ingage and give in Saficiente security by surrenderinge my Selfe
prisonor or otherwise to procicute accordingly : and to Cleare
the Collony from all manner of Charge or Expenses that may
arise in the transportation of my selfe and the Cause from
hence to England and the Charges of it theare : untill the Col-
lonys hands [is] Cleared therof by the authority taking notice
of it theare in what Respect soe Consearning the premised
Differances from this time forward or that is Due to offisses :
&c for since past Touching the premises heare and forther I doe
declare that in truth my Desier of this apeale to be granted is
for the Causses aforesayd and not that I feare any Iniustice
from this presant Court but onene the legallity of ther proceeds
hither unto one the whole matter to them Commetted

John hodson

To our beloved freends John Roome Captayne Richard Morris Richard Tew and Richard Knight the president and Counsell
of this Collony sendeth greeting.

Whereas Ann Elton of portsmouth in Rhode Iland hath
Come before us and Complay[nd] aganst petter Tollman of
nuport in the aforesayd place that hee hath obtaynede in[to]
his handes Craftyly : the substance and goods of Ann Elton
aforesayd and not wi[ll]ing to pay and Retorne the same goods
and debts unto the Sayd Elton aforesayd but at his one will

and plesuer Comsuerves the Substance obtayned by Credett of
the Sayd Ann Elton for his plesuer and Delecatt living aganst
all Reson Equity and good Conscience and aganst the forme of
the Statute of the 7 of Eliz : in that Case made and provide[d]
Therfore this is to will and Requier you the Commistioners
Aforesayd to goe to the place wher the sayd petter Tollman
Doth Inhabitt or Dwell and ther or Elce wher you sha[ll] thinke
fitt in the most Conveniant place to Execute this your Comition
and to Call before you petter Tollman or his wife or any other
parson or parsones whatsoever Dwelling within this Collony
and them Examine upon oath or otherwise wher the monye
goodes Cattle or Lands or howses or any other Estate of depts
of the Sayd petter Tollmanes is or in whose hands it is or doth
Remayne or hath bine since the beginning of november: 1649
and it you shall sease into your hands to the value of 300 li as
alsoe all his negers that are and have bine knowne to be petter
Tollmanes since his Comminge into new England them also
you shall sease: and the Same negers goods monyes Cattle depts
or other Estate you shall aprase untill you have seased into your
hands unto the value aforesayd that Ann Elton may be satisfied
her Just Debt: and by this your Commition you are inactted to
break open and Enter: if peacable Entrance be Denied any
howse or howsses within this Collony Chest or tronke wher any
of the Estate of tollman shall be or is Remayning and thes are
to Requier all officers of Justice Constable or other persones
to be aydinge unto the Aforesayd Commitioners in the Excutit-
ing of this our Commition as you will answer the Contrary at
your prell

Given under our hands and seale of the Collony this first
Day of Desember (1649)

You are to take notice that in the Excicution of this Commition you are to looke unto Sartaine Instroctiones annexed and to performe it accordingly and no otherwise	John Smith president John Sanford Samuelle Gorton William Baulston John porter
Seale	Randall houldon John Wickes

Ther being A Commition presented by John hodson that was granted forth under the hands of John Smith prsedent John Sanford Samuell Gorton William Baulston John porter Randall howldon John Wickes to Commitionatt John Roome Capt Richard Morrice Richard Tew and Richard knight to searve of one the goods or Cattle of petter Tollmanes : it being presented in this Court : the Court doe order that it be kept safe in the Court Roles and Entered one Record in the gennerall Records John hodson paying the Recorder for Entering it.

Ther being A motion presented to this Court by John hodson wherin hee serves for an apeale to be granted him to the kings bench in England : with Respect to the Cause or Causses that Consearnes petter Tollman Ann Elton and himself which motion was presented under his hand the answer of the Court is that they Refere him to the Court of Commitioners for his answer to his motion if hee yett find himselfe agreeved for asmuch as ther apeares : noe Cause to this Court fully to answer his motion soe as to grant the same

A bill of Indictment presented by William harris to the grand Jury aganst William Burton Richard Townsen John Wickes Jun : John ford Rowse helme moses Leppett Roger Burlinggame Ebenezer Moone Thomas Relph george goff John hoowod for Entering forceablely upon his lands and moeing his medowes The Sayd William Burton Richard Townsen John wickes Ju John ford Rowse Helmes moses Leppett Roger Burlinggame Ebenezer Moone Thomas Relph
george goff John hoowod for Entering forceablely upon his lands and moeing his meadowes The Sayd William Burton Richard Townsen John wickes Ju John ford Rowse Helmes moses Leppett Roger Burlinggame Ebenezer monee Thomas Relph
george goff being Called pleads not guilty and puts themselves upon the Triall of god and the Country   the verditt (guilty)

the Jury betwixt William harris and w. of warwicke

Mr Samuell Wilbore	george gardener
James Badcocke	Thomas brownell
John Tripp	Caleb Carr
John Bridge	John Elton
Frances brayton	Frances uselton
Thomas Hart	William Resby

Mr John wickes and Mr Edmund Calverly being bound for William Burton Richard Townsen John wickes Jun : John Ford &c the parsones all apearing in Court the Court doe declare the bonds of the aforesayd Wickes and Calverly to be fullfiled and that they are Cleared from ther bonds

Wheras William harris did Indict for forceably Entrey thes severall parsones (to witt) William Burton Richard Townsen John wickes Jun : and others and Did indict them in his owne name and yett the grand Jury found the bill and they the Indicted partyes Traversed the Indictment and put themselves to Triall by ther peares and a Jury impanelled upon them; but after the Jury weare sworne to bring in A treue verdict the persones Indicted pleaded the Elegallity of the bill of Indictment because not Exhibited in his maiestyes name not with standing which plea the Jury found them guilty and it seemeth Did not mind that plea of waight Saficient to wave such a verdict wherupon the presoners take themselves illegally condemed and Desier that the Court will susspend Judgment aganst them : being his maieste is not mentioned to be the offended party or that ther proceeds wear Contrary to his Crowne and Dignyty but Contrary to the Complaynnant william harris his minde : The Court are not soe Cleare to give Judgment one the verdict. Especially Consederinge that the parsones Crave the favour of the Court that the matter may bee Refered to the next Court of Commisioners to judge of the Legallity of the aforesayd Indictment and doe Ingage to Stand to the determination of the Sayd Court theron Either to be Cleared or Condemned

The Jury on
    Zackry Roade indictment

Samuell wilbore	Thomas hart
fraynces brayton	Thomas brownell

george gardener	James badcocke
Richard Carder	Caleb Carr
John Tripp	William Risby
John Bridges	John Elton

William Burton and Amos westcott being bound for Zackary Rhoades apearance to the Court held at warwicke october the 14 : 1662 : and bringing the Sayd Rhoades forth the Court declare they are freed of the bonds.

In the abseance of the gennerall atornye a bill of Indictment presented by Mr John greene gennerall Asistant aganst Zackary Rhoads for forceable Detayner and the Sayd Rhoads being Called pleads not guilty and puts himselfe to be tryed by his peares

A grand Jury impanelled

Mr William harris forman	James greene
Mr John gould	Edmund Calverly
Thomas Stafford	Richard osborne
Thomas bradly	frances darby
James swett	John gereardy
John swett	Edward marshall

Page 119

Ther being A bill of Indictment presented by Mr John greene gennerall Asistant again[st] Zackary Rhoads for forceable Detayner : which Indictment was Traversed by the Indicted par[son] and the Cause Committed to the petty Jury and they haveing bine upon the Case fower dayes doe Retorne to the Court and leave the matter not agreeing to delever any other verdict then what was before : that was that they bringe in A Speciall verdict and Can noe more meddle with the Cause but must Stand to the triall of law if any will procicute them

A bill of Indictment presented (by Mr. John Sanford gennerall Atorny) aganst margrett Smith the wife of John Smith of Quononnycott for being A pariured parson which Misbehavour of heares is Contrary to the honor of his maiestyes Crowne and Dignyty

A Court of Trialles held at providence march: 10: 1662:
or 63

Mr. Benidict Arnold presedent

Mr William feild gen Asistant for providence

Mr William Baulston asistant for portsmouth

Mr Richard Tew Asistant for nuport

Mr John Greene Asistant for warwicke

Mr Thomas olnye }
Mr William Carpender } Debetes for the towne of providence

Joseph Torrey Recorder

Mr James Rogers gennerall Sargant

Mr John Sanford gen Atornye

THE GRAND JURY

Mr Richard waterman for	Mr Daniell Browne
Mr Thomas harris Sen:	Mr Samuell Stafford
Mr Thomas olnye Jun:	Mr Nathanell waterman
Mr Edmund Calverly	Mr Samuell Bennett
Mr Richard Carder	Mr John Whippell Sen:
Mr Thomas paynter	

The Jury one A Case Depending betwext John Garriardy
and Robert westcott

John Shelldon foreman	Thomas greene
James Ashton	Thomas angle
Thomas Roberts	Thomas harris Jun
william Burton	Thomas hubkines
Eduard Larken	william hakenes
henry Temberlack	Thomas Smith

March 15 : 1662 or : 63

Upon the Consederation of the not agreeing of both grand
Jury and pettye Jury the Court seeing nessestity have thangst
fitt to adiourne this Court untill Tusday the 12 of may : 1663

May the 12 the Court Called may the 14 of may Doe this
Determine

That wheras in the Case that was Committed to the pettye
Jury which hade its being by John Garriardy aganst Robert
westcott one, which the Court have had longe patience and
haveing often Called one the Jury to know if they weare

agreed : ther answer is that ten of them are agreed but can goe no forder : therfore they Desier to be Dismised : the answer of the Court is that the names of the two that are absent be taken notis of which are Thomas greene and William Burton both of warwicke : who have neglected and Refused to atend the Cause : and therfore the Court taking notis of ther offence doe proceed to the hearing of other matters

To vallington whitman depated Speciall Constable for this porpose this 15 of may : 1663 :

Upon the Complaynt of william harris : of providence : in the Collony of providence plantations to this present Court : now sitting at providence aganst Severall parsones for forceably Entry his Lands aganst his will and Cutting his Timber &c : upon which Complaynt Ther are therfore in his maiestyes name Charles the second king of England Scotland france and Ireland and the Dominniones therto belonging to Requier you forth with to take ayd to arest and Bring before this present Court now sitting at providence Thomas Relph Roger burlinggame John horrod Thomas hedgegers Junior John Rice Larrance pinnick and Ebenezer moone ther to bee Examined of the matters Charged of before this present Court : and to be Dealte with according to law hearof you are not to fayle

datted may 15th : 1663   By the order of the Court Signed by
me Joseph Torrey gen Recorder
may the 16 : 1663

The Retorne and Report of vallington whitman Constituted Constable by Speciall order and having A Speciall warrant Commeted to him Reports as folloeth That when hee Came to pauquaback neare the howse hee Sae Some of them at worke at the howse : and Some A little from the howse but when they Sae him they went all into the howse : and hee tyed his horse to the Rowndes of the Ladder and was goeing into the howse : but when I was goeing into the howse ther Stoode thre with ther axes in ther hand and told me that I should not come in I told them hee had a warrant from the Court : they told him they owned him as Constable of providence but not to have any thinge to doe theare   I told them that I was Constituted Constable for that porpose : and therfore Requiered them in the kinges name to obay ther answer was that the king they owned and the Court they owned but they would not come out : but weare Resoulfed to knocke Downe any man that should pry in upon them for ther howse was ther Castle and this was the mine of one and all : I offered them the warrant if they Did Scruple andrew harrisses reading of it ther answer was they would meddle with noe papers hee forder Sayth that ther was noe dore to the howse : and that there was one place more open in the howse to the ground and some of the Roofe was not Covered

The Examination of John horod before the Court sayes that part of what vallington whitman Sayd is true but not all for wher hee sayes : that some of us weare abroade and some at the howse it is true and when hee told us that hee had a warrant for us : wee asked him in whose name : hee told us in will harrisses Complaynt and for forceable Entry : wee told him that wee had not buld one howse to leave it for him to possese without a due progrese of law but the Cour[t] wee owned : and wee did say that noe man should Come but at his perrill : for I had sarvants and worke folkes ther and I Could not leave them : and I came Down the Last night and this morning went to the presedents to know what his plesuer was and sayd that wee Came upon or land peacablely and begune to Build the Last march and wee had now finneshed almost.

page 122

Ther beinge Bills of Indictment aganst severall parsones found by the grand inquest at this Court and the Sayd parsones haveing traversed ther Indictments and Soe are Consequently to be tryed this Court : Butt the Gennerall Atornye having ben Called to procicutte Doth not apeare nor Answer in Court hee being absent the Court are Straytened being put upon the Confederation that the kings maieste and Law may not be Impayred by the partyes Cleering without triall and Judgment nor without the Same Condemed : or without Law unreasonably keept in

Durance Longer then this Court one thes Indictments : The Court upon Considerations of the Sayd Exigents and haveing former practise of these Courts for Example in the Licke Case: do apoynt and Constitute the Gennerall Recorder to Soplye the place of the Gennerall atornye, in the Gennerall attornyes absence this Court

The Jury one andrew harris traverse

John sheldon for	Thomas harris, Ju
James aston	Thomas hobkines
Thomas Roberts	will hakens
Edword Larken	Thomas Smith
henry Temberlake	John Whipple sen
Thomas angle	Roger morrey

Andrew harris of providence being Indicted by the Grand Jury for that hee hath presumed to Excicute an office in aresting Mr John Smith of warwicke being not lawfully authorized therto the sayd andrew haveing put himselfe upon the triall pleads not giulty

The verdict of the Jury
wee finde Andrew harris not Guiltye

Upon the Retorne of the Juries verdict given in Court upon Andrew harris travice in John greene gennerall Asistant Doth Enter his protest aganst Reviveing of it

William harris of providence being Indicted by Edmund Calverly and having Entered his travice Cales one the Court for a triall the Indicter not apearing and noe one apearing to procicute : the above sayd william harris was Cleared by proclamation

You william harris doe acknolidge your Selfe to owe and Stand Indipted unto his maieste Charles the second : king of England scotland france and Ireland and the Dominnions therto belonging the full and Just sume of one hundred pound starlinge payable upon all Demands

The Condision of this obligation is such that if the above bounden William harris shall Either by himselfe or his atornye make his apearance at the next Collony Court held for the Collony

at portsmouth the second tusday in october next ther to procicutt his Charge aganst John Horrod of warwicke for forceable
Entry upon his lands and possestion then this obligation to be
voyd and of none Efecte otherwise to stand in full force and
vertue.

Taken in Court by mee Joseph Torrey Recorder
may 18 : 1663

You John Wickes and John Horrod of warwicke in the Collony of providence plantationes in new England doe acknolidge
your selves to owe and stand Indebted unto his maieste Charles
the Second king of England scotland france and Ireland and
the Dominnions herto belonging : the full and Just Sume of two
hundred pound starling payable upon all Demands.
The Condistion of this obligation is such that if John horrod
shall make his lawfull apearance at the next Collony Court held
for the Collony at portsmouth the second Tusday of october
next ther to answer the Complaynt of William harris for forceable Entry then this obligation to be voyd and of none Effecte
otherwise to stand in full force and vertue
May 18 : 1663   Taken in Court by mee Joseph Torrey
gen Recorder

Upon the Case Commetted to the Jury Depending betwext
John garriardy and Robert Westcott the one of warwicke the
other of aquednesett after long patience of the Court wayting
many Dayes upon them to heare ther Retorne by way of verdict
and haveing noe Retorne Brought in : at the Command of the
Court the Jury was Called over the Last Day of the Courts sitting unto which Call the whole Jury answers to ther names and
weare agayne sent forth and In a short time after ten of the
Jury agayne makes the Retorne to the Court : they weare
agayne Called over : and ten answers and make Report to the
Court : that too of ther Company : being Invitted to agetate
with them to which ther answer was : it was time for Travelers
to goe to Dinner which answer as the ten Sayth was given by
Thomas Greene of warwicke and william Burton did not manifest his desent from his answer but both of them Refused to

atend the sarvice upon which Report the Court Detirmine that ther should be notise taken and Record made of itt.

The name and the Fines of the Jurymen that weare Chosen by the townes—that did not atend the Court of portsmouth Mr William Almye Cristopher Almye grand Jury Lott Strange Adom mott Josuah Coggesshall are fined ten Shellings apeece and Edward Lea if is Excused because hee is nither free of towne nor Collony
of nuport Mr Caleb Carr Mr John Cowdall Mr John Coggessall and John Wood are fined ten shillinges apeace
James Greene fined five Shillinges

Page 125

The proceed of A Courtt of Triall held at portsmouth october
the 13 : 1663
Mr Benidict Arnold presedent
Mr William Feild Asistant for providence
Mr William Baulston Asistant for portsmouth
Mr Richard Tew Asistant for nuport
Mr John Greene Asistant for warwicke
Mr John Roome debete ⎫
Mr John Sanford Asistant ⎭ for portsmouth
Joseph Torrey gennerall Recorder
Mr James Rogers gennerall Sarjant
Mr John Sanford gennerall Atornye
Mr Richard Bulger gen Solisseter

THE GRAND JURY

Mr William Dyer forman	Lefte [lieutenant] John Albro
Mr William Carpender	Mr John Easton
Mr Zackary Rhoads	Mr James Badcocke
Mr William harris	Mr Richard Carder
Mr William Almye	Mr James Greene
Mr Thomas Brownell	Mr Josua Coggeshall

An action of Trespas upon the Case Commenced by Mr William Carpender and Mr Zachary Roads both of patuxitt aganst Mr John Greene of warwicke Damedge three hundred pound

The Juryes Verdict

Wee find for the plainteffes Cost of Court and five pence Damadge

Upon the verdict of the Jury one the Case betwext Mr Carpender Mr Roads and Mr greene the Court orders Judgment to be Entered

An action of the Case Consearing Trespas Entered by Mr John greene of warwick aganst Mr Zackary Roads of patuxett Damedge one hundred pound

The verdict of the Jury

Wee find for the Defendant Cost of Court upon the verdict of the Jury one the action betwext Mr greene and mr Roads the Court orders Judgment to be Entered only Mr william Baulston Desists and Enters his protest

An action of uniust detaynuer. Entered by Mr william Brenton marchant aganst george Blise blacksmith Damadg six hundred pound

The verdict of the Jury

first Consearning land we find for the Defendant

secondly Consearning sheepe we find for the Defendant Thirdly Consearing Debt we find for the plaintiffe Debt and Damedge sixtye one pound ten shillings and Cost of Court

Mr Brenton atornyes pleading for an arest of Judgment the Court orders as folloeth

Ther being A Case Commetted to the Jury which Consearning Mr william Brenton and george Blise and the Jury having ben sent forth after ther first Comminge three times because the Court could not accept of the verdict and they refuseing to goe forth any more the Court are forced to proceed to other business for the presant and to wave that the Jury profesing they Could doe noe otherwise as the matter was stated therfore the Court Doth Suspend Judgment

An apeale Entered by Mr william feild (granted by Mr John greene of warwicke) aganst Mr william Carpender both of the towne of providence Damedge fiftye pound

The Verdict of the Jury

Wee find for the Defendant Cost of Court
The Court grants Judgment to be Entered

The Jury One William marble

Mr John Coggeshall	Phillep Tabor
petter Easton	Josua Coggeshall
Edward Thurston	andrew harris
Samuell wilbore	william harris
Jaratt Borne	william Sarll
Thomas Stafford	Lott Strange

William marble of Boston being Indicted by the atornye gennerall for that hee hath Tumultiously and by force lay hold one the body of John Lewes and Indevered to Dragge him from his habitation &c: and being asked whether hee weare guilty or not guilty so pleaded not guiltye and puts himselfe upon Triall

The Verdict of the Jury
Guiltye

Page 126

William marble of Boston being Indicted for and found guilty a Riott the Court adiudge him to pay a fine of five pound to the gennerall Tresury and wheras hee was Indicted and the bill found by the grand Jury aganst him for Exercising the place of an officer in this Collony without Lawful athority &c: and Refuseing to put himselfe one the Jury for a Triall in the matter the Court adiudge him to Close Imprisonment During the plesuer of the presedent and two gennerall Asistants and by them to be Released if they See Cause: upon the paying the foresayd fine and all other Just Charges and fees acationed by his being heare aprehended: and keept untill hee be at the Descrestion of the presedent and any two gennerall asistants Released from prison : it being Left to them to take such bond of him or security for his Discharging the foresayd fine &c: as they shall Concive in ther Judgmente to be Safficient and forther the Court Leave it to ther Discreastion upon his Releasment out of prisson to take such bond or security for his future good behaviour as they shall thinke meette

Margrett Smith the wife of John Smith of Conomicott being Indicted and a mandamus being sent forth to Command her to atend this Court but answer being made in Court that she was gone to boston before the mandamus came to her howse the Court doe soe far accept the answer mad one her behalfe that they order a new mandamus to goe forth aganst the next Court.

Mr John Briggs of portsmouth seni: being presented by a bill found by the grand Jury for specking words of very great Reproch aganst Benidict Arnold presedent of This Collony and being Called forth and haveing his Indictment Read before him and being asked what he sayd to the bill of Indictment hee Confesed himselfe guilty and Commetted himselfe to the bench. The Judgment of the Court is that John Briggs shall pay unto the publick Tresury a fine of seven pounds and to stand bound in a bond of Ten pound for to be of the good behaviour untill the next Court and presently to pay the fees of this Court Ther being a bond filled wherin Mr william Carpender of pautuxett and John Swett of warwicke stands ingaged in the sume of one hundred pound starling unto his maiestye That Beniamin smith and Joseph Carpender Abiah Carpender Mr henry Ruddick all of pautuxett in warwicke that they shall be of the good behaviour to all his maiestys leach subiects from the 13 of July 1663 untill the next Court held at portsmouth in october and to apeare at the sayd Court next after the Date of the sayd bond and being Called in Court and proclamation being made whether any man Could accuse them of the breach of ther bond : and none apearing to acuse nor to procicut them for the fact for which they weare bound over for the Court doe declare the men to be freed by proclamation
This Constitution should have be placed before

Mr John Briggs being presented by the atorny gennerall at a Court held at providence march the 10 : 1662: 63 for specking many Reprochful words aganst the presedent Benidict Arnold in Saying hee had gone about to subiect the Collony to plumoth &c: and being Called and Coming now before the

Court and his Indictment being Read before him: Confeseth that hee is guilty of what hee is Charged with in the sayd Indictment : and Referes himselfe to the bench Craveing ther favor hee the sayd John Brigge acknolidging that hee hath wrongfully Charged the presedent having noe grownds Dirictly nor Inderectly soe to Charge him

Upon the Case of Triall for Title of Land one the Indictment of william harris aganst John horrod: the Defendant Requiering a demure the Court grant a demur in Case the Defendant doe put in his answer to William harris his declaration now in the presant Court before it be Dissoulved this Evening and the defendant shall soe be Ingaged to Come to Triall next Court of Trialls at newport and the bond on John horrod the sayd defendant shall Continue in force for his appearance ther to answer the Indictment after the title is Tried and that hee now Immediatly Enter his travice in this Court before that the answer to the action : be put in as abovesayd.

Page 214

The proceeds of A Court of Trialles held at nuport march Eight 1663 :64
Mr Benidick Arnold governor
Mr William Brenton deputy governor
Mr William Baulston Asistant
Mr John Sanford asistant
Mr Roger williames Asistant
Mr Thomas alnye Asistant
Mr Randall howldon Asistant
Mr John greene asistant
Mr John Coggeshall asistant
Mr James Barker asistant
Mr william field asistant
Mr Joseph Clarke asistant
Joseph Torrey gen Recorder
Mr James Rogers gennerall Sarjant
Mr John Sanford gen atornye
Mr Richard bulger solicseter

Grand Jury

Mr william Jeffery	Mr henry Temberlack
Mr John Crendall	Mr Thomas Fish
Mr Zachary Rhodes	Mr Thomas harris seni
Mr John nixson	Mr Josua Coggeshall
Mr John Broune	Mr John Easton
Mr Richard Burden	Mr Edword Thirston

The Jury one william harris and John horrod Cose

John nixson	John Cowdall
Edward Thirston	John gould
henry Temberlake	necolas Cotterell
Robert Collwill	samuell hubberd
Thomas fish	James man
Josua Coggeshall	Tobias Sanders

Ther being A Case depending in this present Court betwene William harris of providence and John horrod of warwick and William harris not apearing in parson but his sone andrew doth make answer in his steed and Ingage to stand to and performe all that Concearnes this present Case fully to all Intent and porposses and to pay and to Recive the Court doe accept the sayd andrew harris agent or atornye in his father William harris Roome

An action of Trespas by william harris of providence aganst John horrod of warwick Damedge two hundred pound Starling.

The verdict is

we find for the plaintiffe Ten Shillings Damedge and Cost of Court

Judgment granted by the Court to be Entered

Jury one Mr Greene and Mr Rhods

John nixson	James man
henry Temberloke	Tobias Sanders
Thomas fish	Thomas Ralph
John Cowdall	Samuell Stafford
necolas Cottrell	John pepordye
Samuell hubberd	Josua Coggeshall

Ane action of the Case Entered June 29 : 1663 by Mr John greene of warwick aganst Zachary Rhods of patuxett damedge one hundred pound This Case was pleaded in october and found for the defendant and the verdict of the jury is upon this Rehearing which was Desiered by the playntiffe

The Juryes verdict

we find for the Defendant Cost of Court

Judgment Entered by order of Court

An action of the Case Entered by Mr william Carpender of providence aganst Mr John Greene of warwicke Damadge fiftye pound Starling

The verdict of the Jury

we find for the plaintiffe Twentye shillings Damedge and Cost of the Court

Judgment Entered by order of Court

THE JURY ONE MR RHODS AND MR GREENE

John nixson	James man
henry Temberlake	Tobias Sanders
Thomas fish	Thomas Relph
John Cowdall	John pepordye
necolas cottrell	Thomas harris
Samull hubbord	Josua Coggeshall

Ane action of dept Entered by Mr Zachary Rhods of patuxett in providence aganst Mr John greene of warwicke Damedge fiftye pound Starling

The Juryes verdict we find for the Defendant Cost of Court

Judgment granted by order of Court

An action of Trespas upon the Case Entered by Mr William Coddington of nuport aganst John Smith of Cononicott Damedge Thirtye pound Starling The Juryes verdict

We find for the playntiffe five pound Damedge and Cost of Court

At a Court held for the Collony at portsmouth october 13 : 1663 Thomas Jenninges of portsmouth being Indicted by the grand Jury for Committing fornication with Richard Burdines neger woman and being Called into atend this Court by vertue of a mandamus signed by the governor &c: the sayd Jennings atending this Court in obediance to the governors Command therin Expresed and hee the sayd Jennings Confeseth himselfe guilty of the Charge layd aganst him in the sayd Indictment and Referes himselfe to the bench Desiering ther favour to him The Sentance of the Court is That the Sayd Thomas Jennings hath for much favour from the Court that hee hath Liberty to pay the fine of fortye shilling, to the public Tresurer betwext this and the last day of the gennerall asembly that shall sitt in may next at nuport or Else then to stend to Recieve the punishment that the law hath provided for such a fact

Robert Taylor being bound for his Dafter mary Taylor who was bound to this Court and hear Indicted for Commetting fornication with george hulatt The sayd Robert apearing in this Court and his Dafter being Called to give answer to the bill of Indictment found aganst her for the aforsd fact hee Doth one his Dafters behalfe Confese shee is guilty of the Charge and praying for favor from the Court to her

The Sentance of the Court is that the Sayd Robert Taylor (upon his Request for favour) hath two months time granted hime to pay the fine that the law hath provided for such a fact which is fortye Shillings The Sayd Taylor Doth Ingage in the Sume of fowre pound to his maiestye to pay or Cause to be payd unto the publick Tresurer of this Collony with in the aforesayd time

George hulatt being Indicted for Commetting fornication with mary Tayler Confeseth himselfe guiltye and prayeth for favorr from the Court The Sentance of the Court is that hee hath two months time granted him Either to pay his fine or then to Come forth to Recive the punishment that the Law hath provided for such a fact and in the meane tim to Remayne in the Sargants Costadye

Page 215

The Jury

John nixson	James man
henry Temberlack	Tobias Sanders
Thomas fish	Thomas Relph
John Cowdall	Samuell Stafford
necolas Cottrell	andrew harris
samuell hubberd	Josua Coggeshall

Thomas Durffee being Indicted for selling powder to the Indians and having ben Called and his Indictment Read before him and he being asked whether guiltye or not guiltye : his answer is he is not guilty and puts himselfe upon the Contry for Triall

The verdictt of the Jury is guilty

The sentance of the Court is that the Sayd Thomas Durfee doe pay a fine of five pound to the publick Tresury within Twentye Dayes or Else to be taken by Exicution

Thomas Durffee being Indicted for Specking and uttering words of great Contempt aganst the government of this Collony and being Called and the Indictment Read before him hee Confeseth himselfe guilty and Referes himself to the bench The Sentance of the Court is that for his aforesd offense that hee Stand bound to his good behaviour in a bond of Twentye pound untill the next Court of Trialls for This Collony and not to depart with out leave of the Courte

It is ordered that the fine of five pounds that is Levied one Thomas Durffee the Court doe order the one halfe shall goe to the gennerall atornye and Solisseter to be Equally Divided betweext them

Samuell Legg being Indicted for Committing fornication with Ezable Scase being Called and Demanded whether guilty or not guilty makes answer (by his atornye) not guiltye and puts himselfe upon the Triall

The verdict of the Jury (not guiltye)

Ezable Scase being Indicted for Comiting fornication with Samuell Legg Confeseth that shee is guilty and Desier favour of the bench upon which Request of hers the Court doe accept of Mr Dyers Ingagment to be Responcable for fortye shillings, for her to be brought forth to the next gennerall asembly Whereas John horrod of warwick was Indicted and a mandamus gone forth to Command his atendance one This Court and being Called and Mr Calverly makeing answer to the Court that when hee Came from home hee did not heare of any mandamus and it doth not apeare to the Court Cartaynely that the sayd John Horrod hath seene the Same the Court Doth wave it for the presant

Upon the Judgment of Court one the Indictment of Mr. Briggs of which he Confesed himsilfe guiltye and desiered favor from that Court upon which the Court adiudged him to pay a fine of seven pound to the publick Tresury and to stand bound to this Court in a bond of Ten pound for his good behaviour and being Called in this Court and none apearing to accuse him, hee is Cleared by proclamation the Tresurer owneing in Court that hee hath Recived the aforesd sume
Margeratt Smith

Margeratt smith being Indicted for periury and being Called before the Court and her Indictmen[t] Read before her and she being asked what shee sayd to the bill whether guiltye or not guilty to which Question her answer is guilty and Desier favor of the Court
The sentance of the Court is that John Smith for his wives offence shall pay a fine of five pound to the publick Tresury within Three months time for which sum the sayd John Smith hath and doth Ingage in open Court) and shee to Remayne in an Incapasety to give Testimony in any Case untill shee be sett at liberty by the gennerall asembly

Att a gennerall Court of Triall held in his maiestys name for this Collony of Rhod Iland and providence plantations at nuport the 8 of march 1663:64 soe Called

Mr William Brenton Deputy governor and george Blis black Smith having Chosen Mr John Coggeshall and Mr william Vahan for arbetrators to End all Defferances between them and Mr Benidict arnold governor to be the third man or umpiar in Case the two aforesayd arbitrators agree not they doe both heare by these presance in open Court acknowlidge an assumsitt or Judgment and give full and ample power to the sayd arbitrators or one of them and the umpiour aforesayd to take out of Either of ther Estate to the value of five hundred pounds Starling in lands goods and Chattles for the leviing of ther award and Judgments unto the full parformance of the premises. They bind themselves ther heires Excectors administerators provided that the arbetrators aforesayd or the aforesayd umpire and one of the arbetrators finnish the matter by giving ther award and Excicuting the Judgment betweene this presant 14 day and the last Day of this presant first month Called march in the Sixteenth yeare of the Raygne of our soveraigne Lord king Charles the second &c:

William Brenton   george Blise
George blisse subscribed in the
presance of us
Roger Williames   John Easton

Upon accation of some debate in this Court Concearing the Death of a young neger sarvant to Mr benidict arnold now govenor in the yeare 1661 soe Called and alsoe Concearning the Death of a son of Mr Joseph Clarke now assistant in the yeare 1662 the Court declares themselves fully satisfied in the proceedings taken by the towne of newport and the officers therof to the Enquiers after the Death of the parsones aforesd and that the proceeding aforesayd weare fully availeable sufficiente and unquestonable as to the Clearing of all parsones from all maner of guilt Relating to the Death of the parsones aforesd.

desember 10th 1663 one appeale Entered by Mr William Carpender of pautuxett as atornye to mathias harvie formerly of warwicke aganst Mr John Greene and the sayd Carpender being Called and not attending the action is waved and Cast out of Court

october 28: 1663 ane action of deteainer Entered by Mr William Dyre aganst Richard Lippencott The sayd Dyre being Called Refuseth to plead to the Case upon which the action is Cast out of Court

Robert Collwell Chosen Jury man by the Towne of providence and appearing and Desiering the Court that hee may be Released pleading the sicknes of his familie &c the Court doe grant the sayd Collwell leve to Retorne to his familye and doe Release him from fine
fines of Jurymen

Thomas Layton and John Cook both Chosen by the towne of portsmouth to searve as Juriours and not atending are by the Court fined Twenty shillings apece

John hickes John wood Richard smith Thomas gould being Called in Court all apeare and are by the sentance of the Court Commeted to the safe Costadye of the sargant as presanors and are to be brought forth againe at the Courts pleasuer and wheras ther weare severall parsones bound for ther appearance (to witt) Capt John Cranston Mr John gould Mr francis Brindly Mr Robert Carr and Mr Caleb who weare bound for the appearance and good behaviour of the sayd Richard Smith Juni: Thomas gould John Wood and John hickes that ther the aforesayd Capt Cranston John gould &c: ther bonds are void and they noe longer locked one as bound for the aforesd parsones

Upon the Consideration that the gennerall asembly bracke up and Did not give order that Coppies should goe forth to the townes the Counsell orders that the Recorder shall send forth Coppies to the severall Townes and leve the price to be sett of them to the next gennerall asembly

The proced of a Court of Trialls octobr the 19: 1664 sitting at newport one Rhod Iland in the Collony of Rhod Iland and providence plantations

Mr Benidicke Arnold governor
Mr william Brenton Deputy governor
Mr John Coggeshall asistant
Mr James barker asistant
Mr Joseph Clarke asistant
Mr william feild asistant
Mr Thomas olnye asistant
Mr Roger williames asistant
Mr William Baulston asistant
Mr John Sanford asistant
Mr Randall howldon asistant
Mr Walter Todd asistant

Grand Jury

Mr Edward Smith foreman	Mr Thomas greene
John anthony	Lefte Eliza Collenes
Mr James greene	Mr John Crandall
Mr Edmund Calverly	Mr William weden
Mr William Dyre	Mr Edward Thirston
Mr henry percye	Mr James Swett

october 13: 1663 and action of Trespas upon the Case Entered by william harris of providence aganst John horrod of warwicke damedge 200 pound Starling pleaded in march and the vardict was for the plaintiff Ten shillings damedg and Cost of Court and at that Court a Rehearing Entered by Mr Calverly as atornye to the defendant and being Called in this Court and after much agotationes and debate Concearing the premises the defendants attornye (viz) in Edmund Calverlye withdrawes his Rehearing formerly Entered in open Court

The Jury one Mr carpenders Case aganst Mr Greene

Mr William Dyre fore	henry percye
William weden	Caleb Carr
Richard Tew	Josua Coggeshall
henry bull	Thomas Layton
william Cadman	peter Tollman
Eliza Collenes	petter Easton

desember 10: 1663 ane action of the Case Concearning Trespas

Entered by Mr william Carpender of pautuxett in providence aganst Mr John greene of warwicke damedge 50 pound starling pleaded in march 1663 :64 and the verdict of Jury was for the plaintiffe 20 shillings damedge and Cost of Court which action was Reheard by the Defendant to this Court and pleaded and being Commetted to the Jury ther verdict is wee finde for the plaintiffe two pence damedge and Cost of Court.

Judgment granted by the Court to be Entered

Mr william Dyer forman	Caleb Carr
William weden	Josua Coggeshall
Richard Tew	Thomas Layton
henry bull	John Cowdall
William Cadman	[pette]r Easton
henry percye	[John] anthony

desember 13 : 1663 and action of dept Entered by Mr Zachary Rhodo of pautuxett in provedince aganst Mr John greene asistant of warwicke Damedge 50 pound starling pleaded in march and the verdict of the Jury was for the Defendent upon the same ther was a Rehearing Entered by the plaintiffe to this Court in october and pleaded and Committed to the Jury and the Juryes verdict is we find for the plaintiffe Damedge Twentye pound and Cost of Court

Judgment ordered by the Court to be Entered

Page 217

The Jury one the Case betweene Mr Dyre and Mr Coddington

Mr Richard Tew foreman	Thomas Layton
William weden	John Cowdall
henry bull	petter Easton
henry percye	John anthony
Caleb Carr	Eliza Callens
Josua Coggshall	pelege sherman

September 17 : 1664 ane action of Trespass upon the Case Entered by Mr william Coddington Synier aganst Mr william Dyre of newport Damedge sixtye pound Starling

The verdict of the Jury
wee find for the plaintiffe Damedg 16 pound and Cost of Court

Judgment granted to be Entred by the Court

one the action of Mr Dyre aganst Mr Coddington

Mr Richard Tew	Josua Coggshall
william weden	Thomas Layton
peter Tollman	John Cowdall
pelege shereman	peter Easton
william Codman	John anthony
henry persie	Eliza Collens

September 19: 1664 ane action of Trespas Entered by Mr william Dyre aganst Mr william Coddington Damedge 50 pound Starling

The verdict of the Jury is
wee find for the Defendant Cost of Court

Judgment granted by the Court to be Entered September 19: 1664 and action of Trespass Entered by Mr william Dyre aganst Mr William Coddington damedge 20 pound starling to this action ther was a non sute Entered by the defendant which non sutt was approved by the Court

Septembr 16: 1664 ane action of slander and defamation Entered by Mrs Katherin Milles to william milles late of Boston aganst Ralph Earll seni (of portsmouth one Rhod Iland) damedge 500 pounds starling ane nihil disett Entered by the plaintiffe and approved of by the Court The Jury goe forth to Inquier of damedges

The verdict of the Jury is
wee find for the plaintiffe five pound damedge and Cost of Court

Judgment granted to be Entered
April 4th: 1664 ane action of slander and defamation Entered by Docter alias Capt John Cranston of newport and Rhod Iland aganst one Phillip Reade a stranger Resedent one Rhod Iland aforesd Damedge 500 : pound Starling october the 12:1664 a nihil disett Entered by the sayd plaintiffe and

aproved of but to put ane End to the defferance and to stope farther proceede Mr Roger williames of providence as agent or atorny to one for the aforesd Reade Doth Ingage and subscribe as followeth

Newport one Rhod Iland the 20: of the 8: 1664 soe Called Wheras by the good providence of god, Capt John Cranston of newport one Rhod Iland hath ben in the way of phisick and surgerye a very happie Instrument of much blissing and mercy to many in the Towne and Iland aforesd in which Respect the whole Collony of Rhod Iland and providence plantations hath seene Just Cause by a late publicke Carrictar and Title of honour and Incoriadgment to acknowledge the same and whereas one Mr Phillep Reads a Stranger to this place profesing himselfe to be a phisistion and Chyrargeon'hath lately in and about the towne of newport and Else where Uttered many words tending to the Disparradgment and Discorradgment of the sayd Capt Cranston aforesd at which the sayd Capt Cranston hath ben Justly offended and hath proceeded in a peaceable and legall way for Reparation

I Roger Williames being at the Request of the sayd Mr Phillep Read assigned and appoynted his arbetrator to moderate and Compose all Controversies betwene the sayd Capt Cranston and himselfe doe by these presance publish and declare to all men that I am very much agreived and aflicted at and for the inadvised and Rash the false and Injurious Exprestiones of the sayd Mr Phillip Reades aganst the sayd Capt Cranston and I Earnestly Desier they may be all throwne into the grave of human weaknes and passions to which all mankind is subject I doe also further Engage that the sayd Mr Phillep Read shall if hee apeare agayne in this Collony personally subscribe to this my Detirmination and acknowledgment or otherwise if hee Refuse to subscribe unto it I proclaime unto all men that aforesd Capt Cranston is most Justly free and at his leberty to proceed in a legall procese aganst the sayd Mr Phillep Read for all his grevances aforesd

This for the procuring of peace and love betweene my beloved Countrymen and frends in this barbarous desart as alsoe for

the Incorraging of all worthy actiones and Exprestions and
for the Discouraging of the Contrary I thought fitt to Declare
as my full and finall Determination in the Case Committed to
mee witness my hand   Roger Williames

Whereas in this presant Court a Case depending betwene
docter alias Capt John Cranst[on] of newport aganst phillep
Read formerly Resedent one Rhod Iland bearing Date aprill 4
1664 which action was ane action of slander and Deformation
and the sayd Read not appeari[ng] but Mr Roger Williams
as agent and attornye Interceading with the aforesd Capt Cranston: and to Satisfie the aforesd Capt: the aforesd Roger Williams hath given under his hand the above sayd written acknowledgment and Engagment as is alone written and subscribed as
a free and willing acknowledgment and Consentt that the above
written shall be placed to Record in the publicke Record of this
Collony ther to Remayne Either for the full and absoelute
Clearing of the aforesd Cranston or for my full and free a sent
and approbation aganst the foresd Read if Ever hee Come into
this Collony againe

Page 218

Mr Edword Smith foreman of the grand Jury Requesting
that hee may be Released to goe home being not well upon which
the Court Sees Cause to grant his Request provided hee Come
againe if the Court Sees Cause to send for him

Thomas Walwin of providence being Indicted by the grand
Jury for Committing Fornication with Ann Smith late of providence and having presented himselfe before the Court and upon
the hearing his sayd Indictment Read the sayd Walwine Confeseth himselfe guiltye and Referes himselfe to the bench the
sentance of the Court is That his punishment is to pay fortye
shillings or to be whipt The sayd walwin Doth Choose to pay
Fortye shillings

Mr Thomas olnye of providence Engageth to pay fortye
shillings to the publicke Tresury one Thomas Walwins account
upon which the sayd Thomas walwine is freed by proclamation
paying fees

John Samson and Johanah folgiour being Indicted for fornication and being Called before the Court pleads both of them guiltye of the acte and Referes themselves to the bench upon the Debate whether they Intended marradge yea or noe ther answer is they did Intend marradge by [but] weare hendered by her mother
The Question being asked whether any Did know that Johunah parrance [parents] Did Concent upon which James Rogers gen sargant Doth Testifie that upon Discorse with the mother of the foresd Johanah shee Did owne that shee had formerly given Concent

John anthony being engaged Sayth that upon Discorse with peter folgiour the Sayd folgiour Did aske whether hee Did know John Samson to which anthony sayd noe hee did not know him folgiour farther sayd that hee hade a mind to hes Daster and that hee hee had a Report that hee was a good husband and hee did Intend to looke out for land for him at nantuckett whether hee was going and farther sayes that hee had heard her mother specke to the same porpose that shee alsoe Did give her Consent

The sentance of the Court upon John Samson and Johanah folgiour that the law is to pay fortye shillings or be wipt but they are soe far favorable to them that they Doe for the presant Remitt the Excicution of the law for some Cartaine tim it appearing that ther is a Constant purpose of marridge betweene them

John anthony who was bound for Johanah folgiour: the Court Declare his bonds to be voyd
peter Tollman Doth Recognice himselfe unto his majestye Charles the second king of England &c: in the sume of Ten pounds to procicutt a bill of Indictment that hee hath Drawne up aganst Thomas Durfee of portsmouth and to the full and true performance hearrof hee ownes himselfe fully Content

Taken in Court

Jury one Thomas Durfee bond
Richard Tew fore
william weden

Thomas Durfee being bound in a bond of Twentye pound bearing

James Swett
peledg sherman
william cadman
henry percye
Josua Coggshall
Thomas Layton
John Cowdall
Petter Easton

John anthony
Eliza Collens

Date June the twelfe 1664 and being Called in Court is accused by petter Tollman for the breace of his bond The sayd Durfee plead not guiltye and puts him-selfe upon Triall

The verdict of the Jury wee find Thomas Durfee guiltye.

Grace baylye wife of william baylye late of portsmouth being bound to procicutt James welch and being Called in Court and not appearing her bonds are Declared to bee forfitted
James welch being presonor and being Indicted and Called in Court did not answer

Samuell Dyre being bound in a bond of Ten pound to his majesty Charles the second king of England &c: and being Called in Court and not appearing his bonds are Declared to be forfitted

Robert Griffen being bound to this Court and two billes of Indictment found by the grand jury and the sayd Griffen being Called and the atornye being Called and not appearing nor none to procicute the Indictment the sayd griffen is Cleared by proclamation

petter golden being Commetted to prison for fellony and being Indicted for felony and the Court being Informed that the aforesd peter golden was Rane away therfore the Court is forsed to leave the matter and Cannot proceed in the premises

John gould being Chosen Juryman by the towne of newport and not appearing is fined Ten shillings
gregory Dexter John Throgmorton and anthony Everandeth Chosen Jurymen by the towne of providence and not appearing are finid 20 Each of them
gidian freborn being Chosen Juryman by the towne of ports-mouth and not apearing is fined 20 shillings

Page 219

The proceeds of a Court of Trialles may the 8th: 1665
Mr Benidict Arnold governor
Mr william Brenton Deputy governor
Mr John gard [card] asistant
Mr James barker asistant
Mr Edword smith asistant
Mr william Carpender asistant
Mr Arther Fenner asistant
Mr John browne asistant
Mr william Baulston asistant
Mr samuell wilboure asistant
Mr Randall howldon asistant
Mr John Greene asistant
Joseph Torrey gen Recorder
Mr James Rogers gen Sargant
Mr John Easton gen atornye

Grand Jury

Mr william Jeffery forman	Mr Jaratt Borne
Mr John Cowdall	Mr Zachary Rhods
Mr Richard Tew	Mr James Greene
Mr William Dyre	Mr Barthollmae hunt
Mr Edword greenman	Mr Thomas hobson
Mr Ralph Earll	Mr John gariardye

Wheras Richard pearse of portsmouth one Rhod Iland in the Collony of Rhod Iland and providence plantationes or kings province was bound in a bond of fortye pound unto his majestye for the appearance of Thomas Durffe in the Court of Trialles held at newport may the 8th 1665 and the said Durffe appearing in Court The aforesaid pearce is freed from the aforesaid bond

The Jury one Thomas Durffe being Indicted

Caleb Carr foreman	John potter
John peperdye	francis brayton
James man	Josua Coggshall

John allmye   Robert Stanton
John Cook   peter george
Thomas greene   Joseph Kent

Wheras Thomas Durffe Stood Indicted for felony in taking good from peter Tollman and haveing put himselfe upon the Triall of a Jury is by them found guiltye

The sentance of the Court is that the said Thomas Durffe shall whipe Benjamin wild who is by the Court Sentanced to be whipt and to Recive fifteene stripes and upon soe Doeing the said Durffe is to be freed paying fees

Wheras Benjamin wild sarvant to Richard Dun was in this Court Indicted for stealing severall Knives from Thomas Bruse adjudged to be worth to the full value of one pound one shillinge and wheras the said wild was asked whether guilty or not guilty his answer was guilty and Referes himsilfe to the bench and wheras it Doth appear to the Court that six of the knives Cannot be found Therfore the sentance of the Court is that the 15 knives that are brought into Court shal be Retorned to the said Thomas bruse and seven and Twenty shillings more which is to make up the full sume of Two pound two shillings which is Duble Restitution according to the law of this Collony which is presantly to be payd by the said wild unto the said Bruse and farther the sayd wild is to be whipt with fefteene stripes to morrow at Eleven of the Clocke by this sentance of Court and to Remaine in the house of Corextion untill the premises be performed and the fees Due to offecers paid.

Wheras Nathanell Dickens of newport was Indicted for breace of peace and being Called and asked whether he weare guilty or not guilty he plead guilty and Referres himselfe to the Court The sentance of Court is that the said nathanial Dickens shall pay a fine of Ten shillings to the gennerall Tresurer and pay the fees Due to officers of Court besides and then to be freed by proclamation from his bond

Wheras John havens of portsmouth was Indicted for specking words of Contempt against the honourable his majestyes Commistioners and against the governor of this Collony and wheras the said havens was Called before the Court and his Indictment Read before hime he the said havenes pleaded to the said Indictment guilty and Referes himselfe to the bench The Sentance of the Court is that the said John havenes Shall stand bound in a bond of Twentye pound to his majesty to be of a peaceable and good behaveour to all his majestyes Leage people untill the next Court of Trialles to be holden at newport the Last wensday save one in october next and then to apeare before the Court and Cleared...guillte and farther the said John havenes is alsoe to make a publicke acknowledgment according to the Courts pleasure to morrow about a Seven of the Clocke for his said offence as is alsoe Drane up by the Court as followeth

I John havenes doe acknowledge and Confese that I have notoriously abused his majestyes most honorable Commistioners as alsoe the worshepfull governor Benidict arnold in not only specking aprobious speches but grose falshoods and that Causlesly for which misbehaviouers of mine I am heartyly sorry and doe promise amendment for the future and however it be that the honourable sir Robert Carr hath through Clemacy past by my said offense Respecking ther honour yett I doe acknowlidge the favour of this Court in binding mee over to my good behaviour unto the next Court for that Ignomianous Exprestiones of mine against the governor

Page 220

The proceeds of a Court of Trialles held at newport october 18 : 1665
Mr Benedict arnold governor
Mr William Brenton Deputy governor
Mr John gord [card] asistant
Mr James Barker asistant
Mr Edword Smith asistant
Mr William Carpendter asistant
Mr Arther fenner asistant
Mr John browne asistant
Mr william Baulston asistant

Mr Samuell wilboure asistant
Mr Randall houldon asistant
Mr John greene asistant
Joseph Torrey gen Recorder
Mr James Rogers gen Sargent
Mr John Easton gen atornye
Mr William Dyre gen salissetor

The Grand Jury

Mr william Jeffery foreman	Mr John odlin
Mr Thomas Clarke	Mr Robert Taylor
Mr Jacob mott	Mr Ralph Earll
Mr henry Riddicke	Mr William Cahone
Mr amos westcott	Mr Edword greenman
Mr barthellmue hunt	Mr Edmund Richmund

The Court being Called and soe many of the majestrats being absent of the first Day of the Courts sitting The majestrats that mett adjourned untill the next Day being Thirsday Eight of the Clocke

Thirsday the Court being Called againe and soe many of the majestrates being absent that those mett Could not proceed they did therfore Conclud and agree to adjourne untill to morrow one of the Clocke and in meane time to send for Mr william baulston and Mr John greene that soe by ther Coming the Court may be in a full Capassitye to proceed

Tusday being 24 day The Courte satt

The Court having ben much Excercised by Reson of the absence of severall of the majestrates : doe take notice that the Excuse of Mr arther fenner and Mr John greene have mad are not soe substantiall as to satisfie but doe Leave the Consideration of it to the next gen asembly

The Jury

Mr Edward greenman	Benjamin Smith
Robert Stanton	henry Riddick
Edward Richmund	william Cahone
John pepardye	Ralph Earll

Capt Thomas Cooke   John odlin
bartholmue west   Jacob mott

September 27: 1665 an action of the Case for detaynure Entered by Mr Samuell Elles Living at Millford in the Collony of Conetticott against henry bull of newport Damedge 500 pound starling

verdict of Jury

wee find for the Defendant Cost of Court

Judgment granted by the Court

A Rehearing Entered by the plaintiffe november the second 1665

THE JURY

Edword greenman   benjamin Smith
Robert Stanton   Jacob mott
Edword Thirston   henry Riddick
John pepordye   william Cahone
Capt Thomas Cooke   Ralph Earll
barthollmue west   Edward Richmund

September 16: 1665 an action of Dept Entered by owen higgen of newport against Thomas hart of newport Damedge five pound starling

verdict of the Jury

wee find for the Defendant Cost of Court

Judgment granted theron

Page 226

The proceeds of A Genrl Court of Tryalls Held At Newport the 7th of May 1666

Mr William Brenton Gor
Mr Nicho Easton Dept Gor
Mr Will Coddington Asist
Mr Richd Tew Asist
Mr John Easton Asist
Mr Will Carpenter Asist
Mr Willi Harris Asist

Mr Willi Baulston Asist
Mr Saml Wilbore Asist
Mr Benj Smyth Asist
John Sanford Genl Recod
Mr James Rogers Gen Serjt
Mr John Easton Genl Atur
Mr Wm Dyre Genrl Solic

GRAND JURRY

Mr John Gould foreman	Mr James Blower
Mr Danill Gould	Mr Joshua Coggeshall
Mr Robert Stanton	Mr Hugh persons
Mr John Audlin	Mr John Trepp senr
Mr Barth Hunt	Mr Tho Winterton
Mr peleg Sanford	Mr Tho Mumford

Thomas Roberts of providence haveinge Misdemeaned himselfe in the face of this Court and being called into the Court Doth acknowlidge it was an Error in him and hath promised that it shall be a Reformation in him for the Future and Desires the Court to pass by his Fault therein and therupon the Court do accept his Acknowlidgment

JURYMEN

William Almy forema	Tho Roberts
Willi Reape	Tho Harris senr
Walter clarke	John Cowdall
peter Easton	John porter
Georg Halsall	Willi Heiffernan
Tho Dungin	William Eaton

Upon the Reheareinge of an action of the Case for Detainure Comenced at the Court of Tryalls held in october last by Samuell Eells pla against Henry Bull Defendt The Court haveinge longe waitted on the Jurry sent the Genrl serjant to know whither they were agreed: The Jurry by the number of Eleven peticon the Court for advissed for as much as their foreman hath absented himselfe From them, therfore they cannot bring in a verdict

The Court Considering that the foreman of the Jurry in the case dependinge betweene Samll Eells and Henry Bull, and findinge noe Law obstructinge and a necesity by the statut for us to Expedit Justice for the avoydinge such damage as by Delayinge to putt the Case to Issue have ordered that an other Juryman be Called and Ingaged to suply the roome of the absent Jurry-man The Govornor Doth Decent from the aforesayd act Mr William Baulston Asistand Doth protest against the aforesaid act

Wheras the Court haveinge waitted for the Jurry and they haveinge as aforesayd given their Reasone why they cannot bringe in a verdict to the action to them Comitted the Court cannot See Cause to Disingage them from that their ingagement in that action yett on necessity see Cause to imploy the sayd Jurry men in their emploiment in the Contryes service under his majestie

Page 227

on pearcys indictmt
JURRY-MEN

Mr Tho Harris senr forema	Wm Heifernan
Will Reap	John Cowdall
Walter Clarke	Tho Roberts
peter Easton	Wm Eaton
Georg Halsall	Tho Nickolls
Tho Dungin	John Almy

Upon an Indictment by Thomas Reed of Rehoboth against Henry pearcy of portsmouth for a Suspetion of Fellony for haveing in his posession two Calves and Beife felonously taken from the Sayd Reed The Sayd Henry pearcy Enters his Travers The indictmt being red to the sayd pearcy and he Demaunded whether Guilty or not Guilty pleads not Guilty Referrs himselfe for Tryall to god and the Cuntry.

The Jurrys Verdict Wee finde Henry pearcy Guilty of the charge within mentioned

Upon an Indictment by the Genrl Aturny against John Gerreardy of Warwick for Felloniosly takeinge away a Cow and two Calves from Thomas Reed of Rehoboth.

the sayd Gerreardy beinge Called and brought into Court his indictment was red to him and he Demaunded whither Guilty or not Guilty he owned himselfe Guilty   The Court haveinge Dismist the formen Grand Jurry, and haveinge occassion for another Grand Jurry impaneled

Mr peleg Sanford foreman   Mr Jeffrey Champlin
Mr Joseph Carpenter   Mr Antho Emry
Mr Tho Winterton   Mr Tho Mumford
Mr Barth Hunt   Mr Joshu Coggeshall

       Mr Andr. Langworth
       Mr James Blower
       Mr Clemt Weavor
       Mr John Brigs
       Mr Joseph Lad

on this Indictmt the aforenamed pettitt Jurry served

Upon an Indictment by Mr William Dyre against Mr William Coddington for Utteringe words of Contumacie &c The Sayd Mr Coddington Enters his Traverse, and pleads not Guilty and refers him Selfe to the Cuntry for Tryall
The Jurrys Verdict not Guilty of the charge
The Govornor Decents from the Verdict
Mr William Coddington cleered by proclamation paying Fees
Upon an Indictment by Mr William Coddington against an Indian called Mattash (alias) Robin for Feloniously to have Stolne a sheepe
The Sayd Indian being brought into the Court and his indictmt red and interpreted and he askt whither guilty or not Guilty (owned Guilty) Is Sentanced to be whipt & pay two fould
Mr Coddington being Contented to take eleven pence for his sheepe and the Genrl Serjant James Rogers payinge twenty shillings to the Genrl Treasurer The sentance is remitted
The sayd Indian cleered by proclamation paying Fees
The Court Doe Detirmin the offence of John Gerrerdy is Grand Larcenie, And therfore according to law shall be

Severly whipt or pay Forty shillings : And shall make Double Restitution for what he hath stolne which is one Cow and two Calves (which are Vallewed worth six pownds) unto Thomas Reed of Rehoboth and the two Calves that were seized and now in the posession of the sayd Thomas Reed Vallewed Forty shillings shall be Deducted out of the Sum And if the sum the Beife is Vallewed at in the Cunstable of portsmouths hands Edward Lay be more then what the Fees and Due chargis of this Court amounts unto then the overpluss is to be delivered unto the sayd Thomas Reed and be Deducted out of the aforesayd sum and soe the sayd Thomas Reed is acquitted of his Bonds

Mr William Baulston is Authorized to order the matter about the beife and to pay the Fees and Costs and returne the overpluss

Mr John porter and William Eaton doe Ingage to pay for John Gererady the sum of Forty shills betwixt this and the 12th of June next unto the Genrl Treasurer in good currant pay and soe the sayd Gerrardy is acquitted of his whipinge

Wheras Henry pearcy of portsmouth being as afore-sayd indicted and found Guilty the Court Doe see cause that for as much as the principle John Gererady who Comitted the Fellony being Found and by this Court according to Law Cencured that Court order that procla be made in this Court that if any have any charge to lay against the sayd pearcy in the premeses they be heard otherwise the sayd pearcy is cleered paying Fees

Robert Hazard chosen Jurryman by the Towne of portsmouth and the Court being informed that he is sick his fine is remitted. Edward Enman &c Resolved Watterman chosen Jurry-men by the Towne of providence And Icobod sheiffeild chosen a Jurreyman by portsmouth &c not apeareing they are Each of them fined the sum of Twenty shillings

Page 235

At A Genrl Court of Tryalls Held At Newport the 24th of October 1666

Mr William Brenton Govor

Mr Nicho Easton Dept Gor
Mr Willi Coddington Asist
Mr Richard Tew Asist
Mr John Easton Asist
Mr William Carpenter Asist
Mr William Harris Asist
Captn Tho Harris Asist
Mr William Baulston Asist
Mr Samll Wilbore Asist
Captn John Greene Asist
Mr Benj Smyth Asist
John Sanford Genrl Recor
Mr James Rogers Genrl Serjt
Mr John Easton Genrl Atur
Mr William Dyre Genrl Solic

GRAND JURRY MEN

Mr William Jeffery Foreman	Mr Tolleration Harris
Mr Nicholas Cotterall	Mr Jared Bourne
Mr Thomas Clarke	Mr John Brigs
Mr John peckham	Mr Edward Lay
Mr William weeden	Mr Thomas Greene
Mr Tho Arnold	Captn Tho Cooke

PETTITT JURRY MEN

Edwd Richmond foreman	Edwd Greeman
John pebody	James Blower
John Wood	John Teift
Rich Dunn	mathew Boomer
Robt Stanton	James man
peter Easton	clemt Weaver

An action of Debt by Bond Comenced by Mr Samuell Gorton & Mr Randall Houldon of Warwicke as feofes in trust or Gardions for Benj Barton Heire to the Deceased Ruface Barton of the sd Warwicke plantif against Walter Todd of the sam Toune Defendant Dam: 150 li st. The Issue joyned not Guilty of the charge. The Jurrys Verdict Wee finde for the plaintiffs Debt and Damidge Fower score and tenn powndes starling for the children : and Cost of Court

Judgment graunte by the Bench, Exicution given forth theron

Wheras William Heifferman Heber shearman and Edmund Shearman have in this courte apeered and Declared that they being (by Samuell Wilson apoynted conservator of the peace at petticomscutt in the Kings province) Bound to this Court and there not apearinge any Bonds nor accusations in the Records nor any person apearing to accuse them, they have Liberty from this Court to Returne to their homes

JURY ON JOB HAWKINS CASE

peter Easton Foreman	Robt Hazard
John pebody	John Cowdall
Joshua Coggeshall	John Teift
Richd Dunn	Math Boomer
Robt Stanton	James Man
Edwd Greenman	Clemt Weavor

An action of Accompt Comenced by Job Haukins of Newport plaintiff against Captn Richad Morris of the same Towne Defendant Damage 100 li starll : The Issue Joyned not Guilty The Jurrys Verdict : We finde for the Defendant Costs of Court — Jugment graunted

Ordered that in Consideration of the long atendance of the Grand-jurry the Court doe order that they shall be allowed twelve shillings out of the Genrl Treasury

Upon An Indictment by the Genrl Solicitor against William Long And Ann Brownell of portsmouth for owninge one an other man and wife not withstanding the majestrats prohibition &c

The sayd persons Enter their Traverce, And beinge askt whether Guilty or not owned Guilty.

The Court doe adjuge them to pay the sum of Forty shillings a peece and pay Fees : And also prhibitt their Liveing to gether being not lawfuly married

Upon an Indictment by the Grand-jurry against William Almy of portsmouth for absentinge himselfe from his Fellow Jurriors on the 8th of May last : The Sayde William Almy enters his Traverce

Upon the plea the sd Almy haveing under his hand put in his Exceptions against the sayd Bill : And the Court Viewinge the Bill doe jug that it was not formall according to Law : Butt the court doe Conceive the cause to be of such concernment that they Referr it to the next Genrl asembly : he is to pay present Fees

Upon an Indictment by the Genrl Solicitor against Thomasin Wilky the wife of Thomas Wilky of newport for [uttering] a false oath against Sarah Turner : The sayd Thomasin Enters her Traverce upon the plea she objecting against the forme of the Bill, the Court Veiwinge it juge it not Formal and therfore wave it And she is cleered by proclamation in open Court paying Fees.
Jeffery Champling Being Indicted and in the Court Called Did not apeere and it apearing to the Court that he was Mandamasied and haveing by some of his neighbors declared that necessity in urgant occupation is his Excuse of being absent The Court doe suspend the proscicution until the next Court of Try[alls]

Page 236

Upon an Indictment by the Genrl Soliciter against Thomas Roberts of providence for Defaming Elizabeth the wife of Walter Cunegrave of Newport in saying she was incontinant to her husband and a trator or treacherous to this Collony and a fugative. Traveris Entred Upon the plea the Court Veiwinge the Indictment doe Conceive the charge in the Indictment is not Indictable
Upon an Indictment by the Genrl Solicitor against Thomas Wilky of Newport for incroaching upon the Comon of Newport setting Fenceing upon the same : The sayd Wilky Enters his Traverce Upon the plea the sayd Thomas Wilky in Court haveinge promised and Ingaged that if it Doth apeere he hath soe Done it shall be againe layd downe to Comon and therfore is cleered paying Fees

Mr peter Easton foreman	Robt Hazard
John pebody	Edward Richmond
Josh. Coggeshall	John Cowdall
Richd Dunn	John Teift
Robt Stanton	Mathew Boomer
Edw Greenman	Clemt Weaver

Upon An Indictment by the Grand Jurry against Robert Spink of portsmouth For that contrary to law he did keepe and maintaine in his house Ann Brooman the wife of Thomas Brooman The sayd spinck Enters his Traverce pleads not Guilty and Reffers himselfe to god and the cuntry for Tryall. The Jurrys verdict Wee finde the Defendant not guilty of the charg according to the Indictment The Judgment of Court is that he is cleere paying Fees.—

Upon an Indictment against John porter of pettacomscutt he beinge mandamassed to this Court and in the Court Called Did not apeere. Butt haveinge by writtinge to some of the Majestrats pleaded Debillity of Bodye for his non apearance: The Court doe Referr the matter to the next Court of Tryalls where he is to make apeere the truth of what he Elegith other wise to be proceaded with for his Contempt

Upon Indictments By William Harris of pawtuxet against Thomas Relph, Roger Burlingham, Willi Burton and John Harrud all of Warwick they being Mandamasied and in this Court Called Did not apeere to Answer Therfore the Court consisting of Eight Majestrates seven of them Declared the Indictments against those fower men were Legaly sumoned and ought to have obayed the Mandamasses but fayleing to apeere are delinquants.
Concerninge the Indictments against Tho Relph Roger Burlingham William Burton and John Harrud the matter beinge a Matter of apeale and not Legaly Tranceferred to this Court for Tryall I protest against the sentance of the Court.—

John Greene Asist

Jurry men on Weavers Case

Edmund calverly forman .	John Brigs
Icobod Sheiffeild	Georg Webb
John Teift	Tho Arnold
John Cook	Robt Westcot
Georg Lawton	Tho Greene
John Almy	Captn. Tho Cooke

Upon an Indictment by Bartholomew Hunt of Newport against clement Weaver of the sd Newport for inclossing part of a high-way and Comons belonging to the sayd Towne the sayd Weaver Enters his Traverce pleads not Guilty and Referrs him Selfe to god and the Cuntry for Tryall. The Jurrys Verdict not Guilty : the Court doe order that the sayd Weavor be clered by proclamation paying Fees   proclamation made in open Court

Upon Indictment by the Genrl Solicitor against Richard Arnold and Marie Angell both of providence for Fornication   The sayd partys being Mandamassed, and in the Court Called did not apeere Thomas Arnold apeering in Court in behalfe of the sayd partys Enters Traverce and owned Guilty   Therfore the sayd Richard and Mary are sentanced to pay Forty shillings a peece fine to the Genrl Treasury or to be whipt   The sayd Thomas Arnold ingages the payment of their Fines

Upon an Indictment by the Genrl aturney against Joan Cowdall the wife of John Cowdal lof Newp. for that she did Ausault Beate and Lame the wife of William Wodell   The sayd John Cowdall in behalfe of his wife apeared and Enters Travers and ownes Guilty   The Court doe order that the sayd Joan Cowdall be bound by Recognizance with two suffitient Sureties to the peace and good Behavior and to apeere at the next Genrl Court of Tryalls and pay pressent Fees.

Jurry on Walwin Case

peter Easton	Edwd Richmond
John pebody	John Cowdall
Josh Coggeshall	John Teift
Rich Dunn	Mathew Boomer

Robt Stanton   Clemt Weaver
Edwd Greenman   Tho Waterman

Upon an Indictment by the Genrl Aturney against Thomas Walwin of providence for that he did Asault beate and Wound Robert Colwell of the sayd providence: The sayd Walwin Enters Traverce pleads not guilty and Refers him selfe to god and the Cuntry for Tryall The Jurrys Verdict Wee finde the Defendant Guilty: The Court doe sentance him to be bound in a bond of twenty pounds to the peace and good behavior and to apeere at the next Court of Tryalls and pay pressent Fees : the sayd Bond was taken in Court.

Upon an Indictment by the Genrl Solicitor against Captn Thomas Hobson of Newport for incroching upon and enclossing part of the Comons of the sayd Towne. Upon the plea the Court doe see cause to Referr the Matter unto Mr Richard Tew Mr John Easton Captn John Cranston Mr William Dyre and Lt Joseph Torrey or any three of them to Determine and run the true line of the sayd Hobsons Land and see the sayd Hobson is acquitted paying Fees

John Geerreardy being bownd to this Court in a Bond of Twenty pownds and being in Court Called and not apearing nor any to answer for him: the Court doe declare he hath Forfited his Recognizence

Wheras Epenetus Olny was chosen a Jurry man by the Towne of providence and also a Deputy but not apeering as a jurryman the Court doe order that if he serve not in the place of Deputy then to pay twenty shills other-wise the Towne of providence is fined twenty shillings

Nathanill Waterman chosen Jurry-man by the Toune of providence and Lt Elisa Collins chosen Jurry-man by the Towne of Warwick and not atending the Court in that service are fined twenty shillings a peece.

Page 240

The Genrl Court of Tryalls Held at Newport the 6th of May 1667
Mr William Brenton Governor

Mr Nicholas Easton Dt Gor
Mr peleg Sanford Asist
Mr William Reape Asist
Mr John Easton Asist
Mr Willi Carpenter Asist
Mr Willi Harris Asist
Mr Willia Baulston Asist
Mr Samuell Wilbur Asist
Captn John Greene Asist
Mr Benj. Smith Asist
John Sanford Genrl Record.
Mr James Rogers Genrl Sarjt
Mr John Easton Genrl Attur
Mr Edward Richmond Genrl Solic

Grand Jurry

Mr William Jeffery Fore-man	Mr Vallintine Whitman
Mr peter Talman	Mr Adam Mott
Mr John Cowdall	Mr Gidion Freeborne
Mr Thomas Clarke	Mr William Correy
Mr Robert Stanton	Mr Edmund Calverly
Mr Anthony Evernden	Mr Richard Carder

Wheras Lawrance Turner was by the last Court bownd to the peace and good behaviour and to apeere at this Court Mr William Jeffery and Mr Obadiah Holmes being suretys and the sayd Turner apeered in Court and proclam. beinge made in open Court and none apeereinge against Therfore he is cleered by proclam paying Fees and his Bonds-men: acquitted of their Bonds.

An action of Ausault and Battery Comenced by James Tennant Marrino pla. agst William Smyton Marinor Defenat. Damage: 20 li starll Dated 16th August 1666 and by the defendt Demurrd to this Court

Mr Caleb Carr haveing promissed in Court to stand to and prforme the sentance of the Court in James Tennants Case his Autherety is aproved Thomas Ward haveing Testifyed to his Letter of Aturney The Declaration beinge not formall so as Either the plaintiff and Defendt could agree to joyne Issue or

the Court see grownd how to state the Issue   Therfore the
Court doe see cause to cast the acc. out of Court
An action of the case Damage 500 li Comenced by Francis
Uselton pla. agst Thomas Stanton of Stoneinge Towne Defenat
Dated 16th of March 1666 or 67 Upon the Debate of the matter the Court doe finde that there is not a just returne of the
writt and therfore doe See cause to throw the action of Court
and what Estate of the sayd stantons was seissed is hereby
Releassed
An Action of the Case for Debt Damage 7 li Comenced by
Mr pelege Sanford against Thomas Augur of Tanton in
plymouth Collony Dated 3. Aprill 1667   The sayd Augur being
in Court Called and not apeereinge the Genrl Serjt in his
behalfe owne a Jugment in the case, wherupon the Court
graunts jugment against him.
Mr John porter beinge mandamussed to apeere at the last Court
of Tryalls and he not there apeeringe the matter was reffered
to a heareinge this Court : The sayd Mr John porter being in
Court Called Did not apeere and It being Eleged that he is
weake and dissabled by Debillity of Body : The Court doe therfore order that if he apeere not at the next Court of Tryales
Either by himselfe (or in case he be not able) by his Aturney,
then he shall be proceeded with according to law as A Guilty
person.

Upon an Indictmt against samuell Winsor of providence for
Contempt. The sayd Winsor beinge called owens Guilty and
referrs himselfe to the Bench : The Bench doe see cause to
acquitt him paying Fees
Jeffery champlin of Newport beinge Mandamassed to apeere
at the last Court, and he there not apeering the matter was
referred to this Court : The Court upon the Consideration of
the matter Doe see cuuse to acquitt him he paying Fees.
Upon an Indictment against William chillingdon For speaking
Treasonable words : he Enters Traverce pleads not Guilty and
Referrs himselfe to god and the Cuntry For Tryall

The pettitt Jurry

Mr peter Easton Foreman   William Case

Henry Bull	Danill Greenell
Georg Hamond	Thomas Fish
William Cadman	John Wood
Joshua Coggeshall	John Cowdall
James Mathusan	Bartho. Hunt

The Jurris Verdict Not Guilty: William Chillingdon is cleered by proclamation paying Fees

An Indictment by the Genrl Sollicitor agst Mr William Reape for selling strong Liquors & wine by Retaile the sayd Mr Reape Enters Traverce: pleads not guilty and refferrs him selfe to God and the cuntry for Tryall: The jurries Verdict. Not Guilty The Court dertirmin the sayd William Reape to be cleered by proclamation paying Fees: proclamation made in open court

Upon Indictment by the Sollicitor against Mr John Ward for selling strong Liquors and wine by Retaile The sayd Mr Ward Enters Traverce pleads not guilty and referrs him Selfe to god & the cuntry for Tryall: The jurrie Verdict Not Guilty : The Court order the sayd Mr Ward is cleered by proclamation in open Court paying Fees

Upon Indictment by the solicitor agst Mr Nathanill Johnson for selling strong Liquors & wine by Retaile The sayd Mr Johnson Enters Traverce pleads not Guilty and Refers him-selfe to god and the Cuntry for Tryall : The Jurrie verdict. Not Guilty. The Court order the sayd Mr Johnson is cleered by proclamation in open Court paying Fees

Upon a Indictment by the Solicitor agst Stephen Saveer for selling strong Liquors & wine by Retaile The sayd Stephen Enters his Traverce pleads that his name is not Rightly Declared in the Indictment Declaringe his name to be Sebeer Therfore the Court doe see cause to Wave the Indictment he paying Fees For as much as the Court haveinge Dismist the Grand jurry. and there now apeeringe some matters that was not Comitted to their hands which Concerns this Court to finish and cannot be done wthout a grand Jurry Therfore the Court doe order an other grand jurry to be forth-with impanelled

GRAND JURRY

Mr William Dyre Fore-man	Mr peter Tolman

Mr Nathanill Johnson	Mr Caleb Car
Mr John Waid	Mr Lawrence Turner
Mr Richard Sayles	Mr Samll Sanford
Mr Jerith Bull	Mr Tho Nicolls
Mr Walter Clarke	Mr Tho Winterton

The sayd Grand jurry Returne two Bills to the Court agst John Willis prisoner

Page 241

Upon Indictment agst John Willis prisoner for perjury and breach of prisson: The sayd Willis beinge brought forth into the Court, and Demaunded whether Guilty or not Guilty of the sayd chargis: ownes Guilty and reffers him selfe to the Bench The court doe sentance John Willis to have his Eares cutt in some publick place in the Towne of newport and that the sayd Willis his Testimony shall not pass nor be accepted in any Court of Record throughout this Collony untill the Genrl Asembly See Cause to order other wise and this he is sentanced for beinge a perjurid person For breach of prison the Court doe sentace him to be keept in prison till he pay Fees or puts in good sureties for the payment therof

Upon Indictment agst the sayd Willis for Fornication, he ownes Guilty: The Court doe centance him for Fornication to be whipt with fifteene stripes in the Toune of Newport. The Court doe order that the aforesayd sentances of punishmt on John Willis shall be Exicuted to morrow beinge the 9th instant before noone if wether or other matters prvent not. The Sayd Sentances were accordingly Exicuted publickly in the sd newpt on the sd day

An Answer to the peticon. of Elizabeth Browne wife of Nicholas Broune the Court doe advise Mr William Baulston and Mr Samuell Wilbur or Either to take course in the matter according as it shall be further made apeere for the maintaininge of the sayd Elizabeth out of her husbands Estate soe as the Toune of portsmo may be freed of charg

Upon Indictmt by William Harris Asist agst Benja Hernden of providence for asaultinge Resistinge with force and voyolance the cunstable in the Exicution of his office &c.

The sd Hernden Enters Traverce pleads not Guilty and Referrs himsilfe to god and the cuntry for Tryall: The Jurrys Verdict Wee Finde Benja. Hernden Guilty of Breach of the peace The Court Doe sentance him to pay the sum of fifty shills to the Genrl Treasury and also pay Fees

Thomas Walwin of providence beinge bound in a bond of 20 li to appeere at this Court and not apeeringe hath forfitted his Recognizence

The Court doe order to alow anthony Emery cunstable of portsmouth the sum of 15s for his paines and trouble in aprihendinge and bringinge Mrs Ann Tolman to the Genrl Asembly and that the Sayd Ann Tolman doe pay the Same before she be Released and the sd sum to be noe president for the future

Wheras Joan the wife of John Cowdall was at the last Court of Tryalls found guilty of the breach of the peace and was referred to this Court The Court doe sentance her to pay a fine of Tenn Shillings to the Genrl Treasury and also pay officers Fees

It is ordered that John Willis shall pay Richard Stoures the sum of thirteene shillings fower pence for his Exicuting the sentancis of the Court on him

It is ordered that Ann late wife to peter Tolman shall pay to Richard Stours six shills Eight pence for Exicuting the Courts sentance on her, and also she is to pay all chargis and Fees of Court

Danill Gould of Newpt and Henry Broune of providence chossen jurry-men and not atendinge that service are fined Twenty shills a peece Mr Walter Todd of Warwick chossen jurryman his fine is remitted. John Reed of Warwick chossen jurryman, and it beinge Declared that his wife is big with child and neere the time of Delivery his fine is remitted

Page 245

At The Genrl Court of Tryalls Held at Newport The 23: of October: 1667
   Mr William Brenton Govornor
   Mr Nicholas Easton Dept Gor

Mr peleg Sanford Asistant
Mr William Reape Asist
Mr John Easton Asist
Mr William Baulston Asist
Mr John Greene Asist
Mr Benj. Smyth Asist
John Sanford Genrl Recd
James Rogers Genrl Serjt
Mr John Easton Genrl Atur
Edward Richmond Genrl Solicir

GRAND JURRY

Mr William Jefferies foreman	Mr Marmaduke Ward
Mr Thomas Clarke	Mr Edward Fisher
Mr John peckham	Captn Tho. Cooke
Mr William Weeden	Mr John Cooke
Mr Richard Dunn	Mr Edmund Calverly
Lt Joseph Torrey	Mr John potter

William Willis haveinge Missbehaved him selfe by breach of
the peace and Misbehavior in Court the Court doe order that
he be Comitted to prison by the Cunstables Custody

The afore-sayd William Willis beinge by this Court Comitted
to prison for Misbehavior & Breach of the peace: And he haveinge peticond the Court for a Release acknowledginge his greate
Faileinge therin the Court doe fine him tenn shillings to the
Genrl Treasury. and to pay all officers Fees. And stands Bound
in the sum of Five pownds to the peace and good Behaviour
and to apeere at the next Genrl Court of Tryalls

Wheras James Rogers Genrl Serjant haveinge Misdemeaned
him selfe in this pressent Court by uncivill Expressions and
Carriges upon which he was by the Court Comitted to the
Custody of Mr Thomas Dunging Cunstable: And he beinge
brought before the Court Doth acknowlige that he was Trance-
ported by Drinke, and that he is heartely Sorry that he did
Soe Misdemeane him selfe and hopes he shall not soe doe for
the future

The Court doe sentance the Genrl Serjant to pay the fine of five
shillings for beinge overcome with drinke

The Court doe accept the Genrl Serjants acknowligment and doe pass by his Misdemeanure upon his afore-sayd promise

Samuell Wayte Henry Tibbots, James Renolds and Walter House taken the Ingagement to his Majte in open Court Richard Smyth taken the oath of Alegience to his Mate in open Court.

PETTITT JURY

Mr Edmd. Calverly foreman	Ralph Earll
Jerith Bull	Henry Tibott
Thomas Clemants	John Cooke
Joshua Coggeshall	Walter House
Abya Carpenter	James Renolds
John potter	Gersham Wodell

An action of Trespas upon the Case Beringe Date the 27th of March 1667 Demurrd to the Court Comenced by Mr James Barker of Newport pla. against Mr peter Easton Treasurer, and in the sd Toune of Newports behalfe Defendt Damage 200 li st

The Issue joyned in a Genrl Issue not Guilty of the Charge The jurries Verdict. Wee find for the plaintiffe Damagis Fifteene pownds starll. and Cost of Court

Judgment Graunted and Exicution Issued forth thereon

ON NICHO EASTONS CASE

Mr Edmd Calverly forman	John Bliss
Edward Greenman	Tho clemants
John pebody	Abya Carpenter
Henry Bull	Jerrith Bull

An action of Detainure beareinge Date the second of sept 1667 Comenced by Nicholas Easton junr plaintif against Mathew Boomer of Newport Damage 100 li St

Issue joyned by the Aturneys. Not Guilty of the Charge

Jurries Verdict. Wee finde for the Defendant Cost of Court. Jugment Graunted.

An action of the case for unjust Detainure bearinge Date 19th sept 1667 Comenced by Mr samll Gorton senr and Captn Randall Houldon both of Worwick plaintiffs [against] against

Walter House of Narragansett defendant Damage 200 li starll Whereas there beinge noe Returne to the office of the Arrest of Waltr House the serjant bringinge him into Court and ingageinge the sayd Defendt shall be Responcible the Court give way that the action goe on

The Issue the Court doe Conceive is alredy joyned by the Aturneys which is a Genrl Issue

The Jurry haveinge beene three times in Court and by the Court sent forth At their first coming in they Declared in Court they are agreed and owne that their foreman shall speake for them. The foreman Declares their Verdict Wee finde for the Defendt Kost of Court, and also Declared that the ground of their Verdict was an order from the Honord Comissioners and that they Did not therin Medell with pertickular Titles to land

And wheras the sayd order of the Honord Comissioners bearinge Date the 15th sept 1665 Directed to the Justices of the peace in this Collony and ther beinge two years time Elapsed from the Date therof It not beinge presented to the Govor or any of them but in this instant Court and then by way of pleas betweene plaintiff and Defendant in a pertickular case The Court doe declare that it was Elegally Detayned from them soe Long. And the court upon the veiwinge of the sayd order have seariously purused the Contents thereof and doe not find the sayd Order Consonnant to the Jurry

Page 246

In the Case Depending betwixt Mr Samuell Gorton and Mr Rondall Houldon plaintiff against Walter House Defendant Concerninge Detainure The Court doe Suspend Jugment and one principle Reason thereof is because seven of the jurriors by a writtinge presented to this Court have upon Ingagement charged their foreman under their hands the sayd writinge beareinge Date the 30th October 1667 which is contrary to their charge given not to Disclose one an others Secritts

The Honord Govor haveinge presented to this Court a Letter with a Copie inclossed from the Honord Collonell Nicolls which sayd Letter was opened the 24th instant the Court haveinge purused the sayd Letter doe referr the further Consideration thereof to the next Genrl Asembly

Wheras Mr John porter was by the order of the last Genrl Court of Tryalls (Held in may) to apeere at this Court, and he beinge in Court called did not apeere nor any Aturney in his behalfe The Court doe sentance him to pay a fine of Five pownds, and pay all Fees

JURRIORS ON MR BERNLYS CASE

Upon Indictment by the Generll Solicitor against Mr Francis Breinly of Newport for Sellinge Liquors or strong Drinke by Retayle, the sayd Mr Breinly being Mandamassed and in Court Called apeers, Enters Traverce pleads not Guilty and Referrs him selfe to god and the Cuntry for Tryall

The Jurris Verdict Wee finde the prissoner at the Barr not guilty.

The Court doe order he shall be acquitted payinge Fees The sayd Mr Breinly was by proclama in open Court acquited

Upon Indictments against William Harris, Thomas Harris senr and Thomas Harris Junr all of providence fo Entering on the ground of Benjamin Hernden of the sayd providence and did there with force and Armes Asault and batter the sd Hernden

The sayd parties beinge to this Court Mandamassed and in Court Called apeered and beinge Distinkly Demanded whither Guilty or not Guilty they Refused to give a possitive Answer The Court doe Detirmine that their Refussing to Answer is taken as if they had not apeered And the Court being in a straight Concerninge the Law in that Case doe Referr the matter of passinge jugment till the next Court of Tryalls

Upon Indictment by the Genrl Solicitor against Mr John porter of Narragansett in the Kings province and Harrud Long alias Gardiner for that they are suspected to Cohabitt and Soe to live in way of incontinency : Mandamassis beinge sent forth, And they in Court Called Did not a peere.

The Court upon Consideration of the matter, Not beinge informed that the Mandamasses were Delivered to the persons in time The Court doe order that Mandamus shall be sent forth to them againe to apeere at the next Court of Tryalls where if they apeere Not they shall be proceeded with as Guilty persons

JURY, ON ELIZ. JOSEPH AND SARAH HERNDEN INDICTMT

Mr peter Talman foreman	John Brigs
Edward Greenman	Jerith Bull
Thomas Burg	John potter
John Fairfeild	Ralph Earll
John Bliss	Joshua Coggeshall
Thomas clements	Thomas Winterton

Upon Indictment by Mr William Harris against Elizabeth Hernden the wife of Benjamin Hernden of providence for Contempt
The sayd Elizabeth beinge Mandamassed and in Court Called Enters Traverce, pleads Not Guilty and Refers her selfe to god to god and the Cuntry for Tryall

Upon Indictment by Mr William Harris against Joseph Hernden sonn of Benjamin Hernden of providence for Contempt
The sayd Joseph beinge Mandamassed and in Court Called apeers, Enters Traverce pleads not Guilty and Refers him Selfe to god and the Cuntry for Tryall
Upon Indictment by Mr William Harris against Sarah Hernden Daughter of Benj Hernden of providence For Contempt
The sayd Sarah beinge mandamassed and in Court Called apeers. Enters Traverce, pleads not Guilty and Refers her Selfe to god and the Cuntry for Tryall

Hannah Foster the wife of William Foster of Newport in open Court Enters Traverce to two Bills of Indictments. The Court for want of a jurry Refer the Tryalls to the next Genrl Court of Tryalls. Thomas Feild, Mr John Sayles and Danill Williams chossen jurry men by the Towne of providence and they not atendinge that service are fined 20 shills a peece Clement Weaver chossen jurryman by the Towne of Newport and he not atendinge is fined 20 shills Thomas Lawton chossen jurry man by the Towne of portsmt. and he not atendinge is fined 20 shills The Towne of portsmouth haveinge Chossen

Robert Dennis a Jurryman and he not haveinge taken the Ingagement of Alegience. The Towne of portsmouth are fined 20 shills.

Samuell Wayte beinge by the Court put on the Jurry and ingaged in a Case, and upon an adjournment of the Court he beinge Called Did not attend to Answer, Is fined 20 shills

Mr Richard Smyth beinge by the Court ordered to serve on the Jurry, he Refussing is fined 10 shills

Whereas the Jurry were sent forth with three Indictmts against vizt Mrs Elizabeth Joseph and Sarah Hernden and the Court haveinge waited long and understandinge the Jurry are Dissipated and are not agreed for a verdict The Court doe order that they bring in their verdict to the next Court of Tryalls

Page 248

The Genrl Court of Tryalls Held At Newport the 11th of May 1668

Mr William Brenton Gor
Mr Nicho Easton Dt Gor
Captn peleg Sanford Asist
Captn John Cranston Asist
Mr John Easton Asist
Mr William Carpenter Asist
Mr Samuell Wilbur Asist
Captn John Greene Asist
Mr Benj. Smith Asist
John Sanford Genrl Recor
Mr James Rogers Genrl Serjt
Mr John Easton Genrl Aturny
Mr William Dyre Genrl Solic

Grand Jurrymen

Mr Edward Smith foreman	Mr Richd Bordin
Mr peter Easton	Mr Edward Lay
Mr Tho. Clarke	Mr James Greene
Mr John peckham senr	Mr Edmund Calverly
Mr Edward Thurston	Mr Georg Gardner
Mr Hugh persons	Mr Robert Stanton,

Whereas Georg Way and Daniell Abbott of providence were bound for the apeereance of Thom Walwin and they presentinge him to the Court and Desireinge to be acquitted of their bonds the Court doe Comitt the sayd Walwin to the serjts. Custody till cald for, & the sd way and Abott are acquitted of their Bonds

The Court haveinge taken into Examina a paper presented by Mr Carpenter signed Daniell Abott wherin he seems to Scandelise the Collony in their Loveinge Treatment of the Honord Comrs &c.   And the sayd Abott owninge the sayd paper to be his hand and that he writt it by missinformation the Court doe give him leave till tomorrow Morneinge for an acknowledgment

JURRIS ON CAPT CRANSTONS CASE

Will Weeden foreman	Tho Greene
Will Dewell	Stukly Westcott
John Bliss	Tho Gould
John Scott	Latham Clarke
Jacob Mott	Jeoff. Champlin
Antho Emry	Jarod Bourne

An action of Debt Comenced by Captn John Cranston pla. against the Estate of William Langly of Newport late Deceassed Dated the 27th Nor, 1667. Dam. 20 li Nihile Dicett Verdict wee finde for the pla. 11 li 4s 4d and Cost of Court judgment Graunted. and Exicution thereon

Whereas Nicholas Easton junr was Bound in a Bond of nine pownd for the apeereance of an Indian Calld Robin at this Court and he the sayd Nicholas haveinge brought the sd indian into Court Desireinge to be releassed of his Bond, he is releassed and the sayd Indian Comitted into the Serjants Custody till Called for by the Court.

Daniell Abbott Haveinge in Court presented his acknowlegment under his hand the Court on the viewinge thereof doe See cause to acquitt him payinge Fees

Upon An Indictment against John Greene of Narragansett for useinge words of Contempt he beinge Mandamassed and in

Court Called pleads not Guilty and referrs himselfe to the Bench The sayd John Greene haveinge putt in an acknowlidgment that he is heartely sorry for useinge and Utteringe such words: the Court accept thereof, and doe acquitt him payinge Fees

Hannah the wife of William Foster, beinge charged in two Indictments. to which she Entered Traverce the last Court of Tryalls Butt beinge in Court Called did not apeere. The Court doe order that Mandamus be sent forth for her apeereance at the next Court of Tryalls

Salvadore and Sussanah servants to Mr John Gard beinge Indicted for Fornication, and beinge to this Court Mandamussed and in Court Cald did not apeere. The Court doe juge them Guilty and sentance them to be whipt with Fifteene stripes a peece or pay a fine of Forty shills a peece to the Genrl Treasury

Page 249

Upon an Indictment by the sollicitor against Mr John porter for liveinge in way of incontenancy with Horrud Long (alias) Gardner

The sayd Mr John porter beinge Mandamassed. and in Court Called pleads not Guilty and Referrs him Selfe to the Cuntry for Tryall.

The jurris Verdict. John porter Not Guilty

The Court doe order that the sayd John porter is cleered by proclamation payinge Fees

Upon Indictment by the Solicitor against Horrud Long alias Gardner she beinge Mandamassed and in Court Cald Did not apeere, and It beinge pleaded by Mr John porter that she is sick and ill The Court doe order that she apeere at the next Court of Tryalls. Either by her selfe or Aturny which if she doe not then to be proceeded withall by the Court for her Contempt

Upon an Indictment against Thomas Dorfie for Fornication, he beinge mandamassed and in Court called, Did not apeere yett after apeereinge and Under his hand owneinge Guilty the Court doe sentance him to be whipt with 15 stripes in the Towne of portsm. or pay a fine of forty shills to the Genrl Treasury: and pay Court Fees.

Ann late wife to peter Talman being Indicted for Fornication and beinge in Court Cald did not apeere the Court doe juge her Guilty of the Charge

The Court doe Sentance her this beinge the second offence to be twice whipt according to law or pay a fine of Fower pounds and pay Court Fees.

Upon Indictment against Thomas Walwin of providence for Fornication

The sayd Walwine being in Court Calld apeeres and ownes Guilty

The Court doe sentance him this beinge the second offence to be forth with whipt with fifteene stripes in Newport, and a weeke after, the licke punishment in the Towne of providence and to pay Court Fees.

Upon Indictment against Robin an Indian for Fellony: The sayd Indian beinge brought into Court Ownes Guilty.

The Court doe Sentance him to be forth with whipt with 15 stripes and pay Fees.

Upon an Indictment against peter Talman of portsm for breach of the peace, and he beinge bound to this Court and in Court Calld apeers, pleads not Guilty and Referrs himselfe to the Bench The Court haveinge heard what the sayd Talman could plead for himselfe: Doe juge him Guilty The Court doe fine him the sum of thirty shillings where of 10s: to the Genrl Treasury and 20s, to the Cunstable Mr John Brigs and also pay court Fees.

Whereas there was three Indictments Delivered to the hands of the jurry vizt Mr peter Ta[lman] foreman &c. and not returneinge a verdict to the Court in October last. It was thereupon Referred to this Court, and they beinge in this Court Calld severall of them did not apeere yett the fore-man with some others apeereinge and answeringe, the fore-man Returnes the papers to him Delivered with a verdict as afirmeth was by the joynt agreement of the whole jurry Drawne up serjt. James Rogers doth in Court Testify that the jurry whereof peter

Talman was foreman on the three Indictments That before the sayd jurry dissapated they unanimosly declared they were agreed of a verdict, whereupon he permitted them to goe to their Lodgings

The Recorder is Ordered to Receive the papers into his hands William Willis beinge by the last Court of Tryalls Held Octor: 1667 bound to the peace and good behavior and to apeere at this Court and beinge in Court Calld apeeres. The sayd Willis haveinge Misbehaved himselfe. by useinge words Rebuking an officer of the Court The Court doe comitt him to the serjants Custody, The sayd Willis haveinge made his acknowledgment under his hand the Court doe Release him out of prison, And his former Bonds are Continewd untill the next Court of Tryalls

Wheras there was a warrant sent from some of the Majistrates to the Cunstable of providence Resolved Watterman for the aprihendinge of William Ward and Ann Brooman and bring them unto this Court: And the sayd Cunstable haveinge made returne to the Court that he is Denyed of ayd in aprihendinge the sayd parties this Court doe referr the further Care and proceed of the matter to the Majestrates on the maine

William Harris beinge in this Court Indicted Came into Court and Enters Traverce

Martha Lay the wife of Edward Lay Doth before the Court beinge Ingaged profes that She still is in feare of her life of Mr Talman and feares that at some time other he will murther her

Whereupon the sayd Mr petter Talman is Bound in the sum of twenty pownds to the peace and good behavior and to apeere at the next Court of Tryalls

John Whiple junr and Epenetus Olney chossen jurry-men by the Towne of providence and they not atendinge that service are fined Each 20s

Page 250

The Genrl Court of Tryalls Held At Newport the 21t Day of October 1668
Mr William Brenton Govor

Mr Nicholas Easton Dt Gor
Captn peleg Sanford Asist
Captn John Cranston Asist
Mr John Easton Asistant
Mr William Carpenter Asist
Mr William Harris Asist
Mr Thomas Harris Asist
Mr William Baulston Asist
Mr Samuell Wilbur Asist
Captn John Greene Asist
Mr Benja Smith Asist
John Sanford Genrl Recor
Mr James Rogers Genrl. serjt.
Mr John Coggeshall Genrl Treas
Mr John Easton Genrl Atury
Mr William Dyre Genrl Solic.

GRAND-JURRY-MEN INGAGED

Mr Joseph Torrey Fore-man	Captn Thomas Cooke
Mr Caleb Carr	Mr Thomas Fish
Mr Climt Weaver	Mr John peckham senr
Mr Thomas Clarke	Mr Edmund Calverly
Mr Henry Bull	Mr Ralph Earll
Mr John Cowdall	Mr Thomas Brooke

Tawpawmisson An Indian beinge Drunk and haveinge broken some glass belonginge to the house in which phillip Eads now Inhabitts. The Court doe Comitt him the sd Indian to the stocks and from thence to prisson till Calld for. The sayd Indian beinge brought before the Court, the Court doe Release him paying Fees

For-as-much as the Court and Cuntry have bene long Detained from proceedinge Upon action all Causes to their great trouble and charge. by Reason that the Grand Jurry cannot agree together to Deliver in the Bills. and whereas pleaders and others concerned in actions are upon the Grand-jurry Therefore the Court thinke not meet as yett to Dismiss the Grand-jurry, but are willinge to permit the parties Concerned in the

actions or Tryalls to plead or speake to the matters in Court.
October 27th the Court adjourned till Munday next which will
be the 2 of Novemb
November 2 the Court Calld and then the Govor was pressent,
Novembr 3 the Grand-jurry Returnd Eight Bills.
The 4th of Nov. 1668 wheras an action was by Mr Samuell
Gorton senr & Mr Randall Houldon both of warwick comenced
against Mr Richard Smith of Narragansett and in bar of the
sd action the defendt saith that the plaintiffs doe not declare
where the sayd Land lies (but in the Narragansett Cuntry) &
soe cannot Answer therto— And that the Kings Comissioners
did order that the Inhabitants of the Narragansett Cuntry
should keep their posessions in peace Untill his Majestys pleasure be further Knowne, and produced the sayd order under
their seales in the Court Wee therfore this Court declare that
the fore-sayd by the Defendant offered as a bar is a lawfull bar
to be Soe Entered of Record
Wee the members of the Court of Tryalls Held for the Collony
at Newport the 21t of October 1668 haveinge perussed a writtinge beareing Date the 4th of Novemr 1668 which writtinge
puts a barr to the action of Mr Samuell Gorton senr & Mr
Randall Holdon plaintiffs &c, wee whose Names are under written doe declare our dessent therunto some of us haveinge also
heard the Govor. in the pressent Court declare his resolution to
have justice proceed in the matter, although by some Occassion
well knoune to the Court he is at pressent abssent from the
Court; The grownds of our Dessent are that wee are not free
to Neglect or Deferr justice Either in this or any other matter
least therby his Majestys graunt should be called in question

William Baulston Asist   John Greene Asist
Samuell Wilbur Asist   Benj. Smith Asist

I doe declare that wheras It is Concluded by some of the Court
that that act of his Majestys Comissioners Is a barr in law: I
say it is noe barr as to hinder any proceedings of the Court in
any matter or thing whatsoever in the Kings province. Delivered in Court the 5 of November 1668 By me William Carpenter
Asistant

Wheras there was an action Called in Court dependinge betweene Collonall Edmund Scarbrough plaintiff and Mr Joseph Holderbee Defendant and they beinge Called the Defendt Disowned, the Letter of Aturney produced in Court by Mr Bartholmew, Stretton, in behalfe of the sayd Scarbrough for as-much as there was neither a publick Nottarys hand or wittneses Viva Voce to Demonstrate the truth therof Therfore the Court cannot see cause to accept of it and soe the action Falls.

JURRY-MEN

William Weeden forman	Jeremiah Willis
Thomas Harte	John Vahan junr
Robert Stanton	James Man
Nathanill Dickins	James Blower
Thomas Watterman	Edward Lay
Danill Gould	Ralph Earll

An action of Trespas beareinge Date the 16th sept 1668. Comenced by Mr William Coddington plaintiff against James Rogers Genrl. serjt. Defendant

The Issue joynd. a Genri. Issue: jurris Verditt Wee find for the plaintiff Damege three pownds twelve shillings and Cost of Court. The Court graunt judgment thereon

Upon an Indictment by the solicitor in Octor: 1666. against Horrud Long (alias) Gardner she being Mandamossed and in Court Cald did not apeere: And after Mr John porter apeereing with a paper signed Horrud Long the Court doe owne him her Aturney: the sayd Mr porter in her behalfe: pleads Not Guilty of Liveinge in incontunancy and Refers her Tryall to god and the Cuntry

The Juris verdict - Horrud Long not Guilty by punktual Testimonys: Jugment Graunted:

The sayd Horrud Long cleered by proclamation in open Court payinge Fees

JURRY-MEN ON HORAD LONGS CASE

William Weeden Foreman	Jer. Willis
Robt Stanton	John Vahan junr
Nath. Dickins	James man

Tho Watterman	Jos. Torrey junr
Danill Gould	Edward Lay
Walter Clarke	Bartho. Hunt

William Willis beinge at the last Genrl Court of Tryall Held in May, bound in a bond of Five pownds to the peace and good behavior at to apeere at this Court, he beinge in Court Called apeers: proclamation beinge made in open Court and none apeeringe to accuse him he is acquitted paying Fees

Hannah, the wife of William Foster of Newport beinge by the Solicitor Indicted in two Bills for Fornication and adultery and beinge to this Court Mandamassed, and in Court Called. Did not apeere

The Court Doe order that she shall be whipt with Fifteene Stripes in the Towne of Newport or pay the sum of Forty shillings to the Genrl Treasuror,

JURRIOS ON MR HARRIS CASE

Will. Weeden fore-man	Jer. Willis
Robt Stanton	John Vahan junr
Nath Dickins	James man
Danll Gould	James Blower
Walter Clarke	Relph Earll
	Jos Torrey junr

Upon Indictment by the Genrl. Solicitor against Mr William Harris for Misbehavior and Contempt of Authorety Beinge in Court Called apeers Enters Traverce: pleads Not Guilty and Referrs himselfe to the Cuntry for Tryall The jurris Verdict (beinge by the Court three times sent forth) Not Guilty, Jugment by the Court Entred The sayd Mr William Harris is in open Court Freed by proclamation paying Fees:

Wheras Mr peeter Talman of portsm. was by the Court of Tryalls in May last bound to the peace and good Behavior and to apeere at this Court and he beinge in Court Called apeeres. And upon the Consideration of the matter this Court doe See Cause to Continew his Bonds to the next Court of Tryalls

Page 253

Wm Weeden foreman	Jer. Willis
Rt Stanton	John Vahan junr
John Greene	James Man
Tho Watterman	Ralph Earll
Danill Gould	Ed Lay
John Cowdall	Barth Hunt

Upon Indictment by the Genrl Solicitor against Mathew Boomer of Newport for Comittinge of a Riott, he beinge Mandamassed apeers in Court Enters Traverce pleads Not Guilty and and Referrs him selfe to the cuntry for Tryall The jurris Verdict (beinge by the Court thre times sent forth) Not Guilty of a Riot by any punctuall Testimony: The Court Enter Jugment, and Mathew Boomer is cleerd by proclamation paying Fees

Thomas Flunders beinge Indicted for Contempt of Authorety and beinge bound over unto this Court and in Court Calld apeeres, and beinge demaunded Whether Guilty or not. Ownes Gulty and Referrs, him selfe to the Bench, The Court upon his acknowlidgment doe acquitt him payinge Fees

Henry Stevens of Newport beinge bound to this Court and Indicted for Adultery, and being in Court Calld apeers, Enters Traverce, pleads Not Guilty and Referrs him Selfe to the Cuntry for Tryall

The Jurris Verdict (Not Guilty of Adultery) the Court Enter Jugment and he is cleerd by proclama. in open Court payinge Fees:

NAMES OF THE JURRY

Willia Weeden fore-man	Jer Willis
Robt Stanton	John Vahan junr
Nath. Dickins	James Man
Tho Waterman	Jos Torrey junr
Danill Gould	Edward Lay
Walter Clarke	Tho Mumford

Upon an Indictment against Thomas Drinkwatter for the illegal and unlawful burneinge a fence of Mr Wm Brentons he beinge bounde over unto this Court and in Court calld apeers Enters Traverce pleads not Guilty and Referrs him selfe to god and the Cuntry for Tryall The Jurris Verdict (Not Guilty) The Court Enters Jugment, cleerd by proclamation payinge Fees

JURRY-MEN

William Weeden	John pebody
Tho Harte	Edw. Greenman
Jer Willis	Tho Nicolls
John Vahan junr	John Greene junr
James Man	Geo Hamond
Tho Watterman	John Odlin

Upon an Indictment against Edward Hodgman for the illegal and unlawful burneinge of a fence belonging to Mr William Brenton of Newport Esqur the sayd Hodgman beinge bound over unto this Court and in Court Called apeeres Enters Traverce pleads not Guilty and Referrs him selfe to the Cuntry for Tryall

The Juris Verdict (not Guilty) The Court Enters Jugment cleerd by proclamation paying Fees

Upon Indictment by the Genrl Solicitor against Elen Boomer the wife of Mathew Boomer of Newport for a Fellony, the sayd Elin being Mandamassed and in Court Calld her husband Mathew Boomer Answered in her behalfe. and Enters Traverce pleads not Guilty, and Referrs her Tryall to the Cuntry

The Jurris verdict (Not Guilty) the Court Enters Jugment, she is cleerd by proclomation paying Fees

NAMES OF THE JURY

Willia Weeden foreman	Jer Willis
Tho Harte	John Vahan junr
Robt Stanton	James Man
Nath. Dickins	Edward Lay
Ralph Earll	Josh Coggeshall
Tho Watterman	Bartho. Hunt

Upon an Indictment against William Aires and Judith his wife, by the Genrl. Solicitor for Breach of peace The sayd persons beinge bound over to the Court and in Court Called apeere Enter

Traverce plead not Guilty and Referr them Selves to god and the Cuntry for Tryall. The Jurris Verdict (Guilty): The Court doe Sentance them to pay three shills fower pence a peece and pay Fees-

JURYMEN ON ARES CASE

William Weedn	Jer Willis
Robt Stanton	John Vahan junr.
Tho Hart	James Man
John Greene	Edw Lay
Tho Watterman	Josh Coggeshall
Danll Gould	Barth Hunt

Elizabeth Stevens the wife of Henry Stevens of Newport beinge sollemly Ingaged accordinge to law in open Court Doth Testify and Declare that she is and stands in feare of her life of her sayd Husband Henry Stevens and desiers Releife from this pressent Court therein Whereupon the sayd Henry Stevens is bound in a Bond of 20 li starll- to be of peaceable and good behavior unto All his Majesties Leige people and more Especially to Elizabeth his wife and to apeere at the next Genrl. Court of Tryalls.

Ambross Leach of Narragansett beinge bound to the peace and good behavior and to apeere at this Court And he beinge in Court Calld did not apeere. the Court upon the Consideration of the matter doe see cause to Continew his Bonds to the next Court of Tryalls
Benjamin Hernden of providence beinge bownd to the peace and good Behavior and to apeere at this Court. And he beinge in Court Calld did not apeere: The Court doe See cause to Continew his Bonds till the next Court of Tryalls
Sarah Greene beinge bound to apeere at this Court - and in Court Called did not apeere
Samll Wayte beinge bound for the apeereance of Sarah Greene. the Court doe See Cause to acquitt him of his Bonds
Isack Bump beinge imprissoned and in this Court indicted for Fornication, he beinge in Court Calld did not apeere the serjant in the Court declares he hath made an Escape.

Ursla the wife of John Cole of charlestowne being Indicted for useinge words of contempt she beinge in Court Cald did not apeere

William Haukins, John Smith Miller, John steere and Joseph Williams chosen Jurry-men by the Toune of providence and they not atendinge that service are fined twenty shills apeece. Thomas Lawton chosen jurry-man by portsmouth fined twenty shills
Tho Cornell and Francis Brayton chosen jurry-men by portsmouth. Fined teen shillings a peece

Page 259

A gennerall Court of Trialles held at newport one Rhod Iland for the Collony of Rhod Iland and providence plantationes may the Tenth 1669
Mr Benedick Arnold governor
Mr John Clarke Deputye governor
Capt John Cranston asistant
Capt peleg Sanford asistant
Mr John Easton asistant
Mr William Carpender asistant
Mr William harris asistant
Mr Thomas olnye Ju: asistant
Mr William Baulston asistant
Mr Josuah Coggshall asistant
Mr Benjanan Smith asistant
Capt John Greene asistant
Joseph Torrey Recorder
Mr James Rogers gen sargant
Mr John Coggshall gen Tresurer
Mr John Easton gen: atornye

GRAND JURY

Mr Caleb Car	Mr John anthony
Mr Edword greenman	Mr John Cowdall
Mr Robert stanton	Mr Jeffery Champian
Mr walter Clarke	Mr Joseph Clarke Ju:

John whippell   Mr Ralph Earll
Mr Edword Lay   Mr John Sayles

may the 7: 1668 John garriardye plaintiffe against Collonell Edmund Scarbrough in an action of Dept Damage two hundred pound starling Demured by the Defendants atornye Mr William smiton untill the Court in may and was then pleaded

The verdict of the Jury

wee find for the plaintiffe seventye two pound Eleven shillings and a penny and Cost of Court

may the 18: 1669 a Rehearing Entered by the Defendants atorny Mr Smiton

The Jury one the Action between Mr Sanford and henry underwood

Edword Richman   Daniell greenell
John greene   gersham wodall
John wood   John gorton
Edword Thirston   John whippell
andrew harris   Thomas fry
adom mott   John Odlyn

aprill 13: 1669 Capt peleg Sanford plaintiffe against henry underwood in ane action of Trespas on the Case Damage 200 pound sterling pleaded and the

verdict of the Jury

wee find for the Defendant Cost of Court not any way touching the title of Land

William Smiton having presented severall Letters of atornye from the Colonell Edmund Scarbrough of verginnia hee is by the Court owned to be his Lawfull atornye to answer to the Complaint of John garriardye against the Estate of Collonell Edmund Scarbrough ordered that a Letter be from the Court sent to Mr William Reape to Request him to Come before the Court and to bring with him those papers spoken of by Mr Smiton into this Court

William ayres of narragansitt Came before the Court and did declare that hee had Retayned Mr John Sanford his atornye to plead his Cause or Causes against Ambross Leach which was

aproved of in Court The above said Leach being Called before
the Court Did Contemtiously Exprese himselfe against the
govenor and alsoe the Court in gennerall and alsoe by the
motiones of his body behave himselfe soe unseemly which gave
the Court Just offence therfore was bound as followeth
you ambras Leach Living at narragansitt in the Collony of
Rhod Iland and providence plantationes or Kings province doe
owne your Selfe Indepted unto his majestye Charles the second
King of England scotland france and Ireland &c: the full and
Just sume of Fortye pound starling to be Levied upon my
Lands good and Chattels and to the true performance therof
you bind your Selfe your heires and assignes firmly by this
promace this 12 day of may 1669 and in the 21 yeare of his
majestyes Raygne The Condistion of the abovesaid obligation
is such that if you the above bounden ambras Leach shall make
your personall appearance at the next gennerall Court of Trialles
held for this Collony the Last wensday save one in october
next and then to appeare before the Court and not to Depart
without the Leave of the Court and in the meane time to be of
good behaviouer to all his majestyes Leach people and in the
mean time not to Imbasell your Estate then this obligation to be
voyd and of none Efect otherwise to stand in full force and
vertue

Taken in Court

henry Stevens being bound, to this Court and being Called and
not appearing the Court sees Cause to Continue his bonds
  Sarah greene alias flownders being bound to the Last Court
and being then Called did not appeare and being now Called and
not appearing the Court orders the aforesaid sarah to be summonsed in to appeare at the next genneral Court
Benjjaman herenden of providence being bound to the Last
Court and being Called then did not appeare was bound to this
Court and being Called doth not appeare The Court sees Cause
to Continue his bonds to the next Court.
uzsala Cole the wife of John Cole of Charles Towne being
bound to the Last Court in a bond of ten pounds and being
Called did not appeare and being called againe in the Court and

not appearing the Court declare the aforesaid bond to be forfitted

Page 260

Wheras many complaints have ben presented befor us by Mr Samuell Wilson Conservator of his majestyes peace in the narragansitt or kings province as his Retorne as to his said office and others alsoe against John Carr somtimes ther Residing as his notorious breaches of the peace and haynous outragous misbehaviours proved by severall afidavids according to the said Complaints to the manifest Danger of the Kings Leach subiects and the great unsurtye and unsaftye of the Lives and Estates &c wee doe Therfore order that the said John Carr shall be Committed to the gennerall Sarjant to be Imprisoned in the Common goall and ther safly to be Kept untill the next Court of Trialles on the Last wensday in october next provided nevertheless that if hee the said Carr have or will procure two sufitient Surtyes freemen of this Collony that will and doe give two hundred pound bond to our Lord the King and his successors that the said Carr shall then and ther appeare and abid the Judgment of the Court and in the mean time be of good behaviour that then the Governor or deputye governor or two asistants upon such said surtyes shall and may Lett to bayle and maine prise the said Carr untill the said Court &c foras much as the grand Jury was discharged before the Complaints were brought forth and being gon home the Court in no Capassitye to Impanill an other grand Jury

Wheras abiah Carpenter and Job almye were Chosen by the Towne of warwicke to atend this Court for to be on the grand Jury and they not appearing and the Court being Informed that the said abiah Carpenter was Constable of the Towne of warwicke and the said almye not being a freeman nether of the Towne of warwicke nor of the Collony The Towne of warwicke is fined by the Court fortye shillings to the publicke Tresury for not observeing the Law in that Case provided

Wheras Mr Joseph Clarke was Chosen by the Towne of newport to be on the grand Jury and not appearing The Court

Considering the matter and how much hee hath ben Imployed formerly and that in this Court his son Joseph was prevayled with to Saply the place of a grand Jury man The Court doe Remitt the aforesd Mr Joseph Clarkes fine for not appearing George hallsall being Chosen by the Towne of warwicke for a Jury man and hee not appearing is fined 20 shillings by the Court

Page 261

The proceeds of A gennerall Court of Trialles sitting at newport october the 20: 1669
Mr Benidict Arnold governor
Mr John Clarke Deputye governor
Capt John Cranston asistant
Capt peleg Sanford asistant
Mr John Easton asistant
Mr William Carpenter asistant
Mr william harris asistant
Mr Thomas olnye Ju: asistant
Mr william Baulston asistant
Mr Josuah Coggeshall asistant
Mr Benjamin Smith asistant
Capt John greene asistant
Joseph Torrey gennerall Recorder
Mr James Rogers gennerall Sargant
Mr John Coggshall gennerall Tresurrer
Mr John Easton gennerall atornye

THE GRAND JURY

Mr Thomas Cornall	Mr Ralph Earll
Mr John gould	Mr Thomas Burg
Mr Robert Stanton	Mr Thomas waterman
Mr george gardner	Mr anthony Emarry
Mr Thomas Clarke	Mr John Cooke
Mr Thomas arnold	Mr James Case

Wheras it doth appeare that ther is a defferance in the Towne of providence about the Choyce of Ther Juriares that Should

have atended This Court: The Court doe Judge that the persones presented by henry brown Cannot be approved of as
Legally Chosen

The grand Jurry Coming Into Court and one of them (viz)
Mr Thomas Arnold declaring in open Court That on a bill that
was presented to them hee Could not agree with his fellowes
because that Mr William Carpenter and Mr william harris and
Mr Thomas olnyes father were Concearned in it and wee sayes
hee are oppositts and farther argued that the Grand Jury were
the majour part of the Court and therfore nothinge ought by
Law to Come to the grand Jury but by ther Consent which
Resoning of his seemed to be soe Redickelous as declared him
to be unsutable to serve on the grand Jury and Therfore was
by the Court take[n] of and Thomas fry put in his Roome to
finish any farther busines that Concernes the grand Jury in
this Court.
1668 may the 7 John garreadye plaintiffe against Collonell
Edmund Scarbrought in an action of dept damage 200 pound
demured at october Court following and pleaded may the tenth
1669 verdict of Jury wee find for the pliantiffe seventye two
pounds Eleven Shillings and a peny and Cost of Court: may
the 18: 1669 a Rehearing Entered by the defendants atornye
Mr william Smitton and pleaded in the Court and the verdict
of the Jury is after the Issues agreed on by the Court (because
the atornyes Could not or had not) is In the Case betweene
John garrardye plaintife Collonell Edmund Scarbrou defendant
The atornyes not agreeing upon the Issue or poynts of Issue
in the Case the Court find it of absolute necestitye to state the
poynts of the Issue which in Efect are Joyned with declaration
and answer which appeares to bee two fold that is first whether
the Tobacco attached were the Estate of the said Scarbroues
and secondly whether hee bee In Depted or how far Indepted to
the said garrardye aforesaid and soe Committed after plea
theron to the Jury and the verdict followes
Wee find for the Defendant Cost of Court
november 14: 1668 an action of Dept upon bill Commenced
by frances Brendly against Robert westcott dept and damage

20 li demured in may and now Joynes Issue and plead to it the
Issue is That the Defendant ownes the Dept was Due but plead
that hee hath by a Colaterall agreement tendered pay according
therto

The verdict of the Jury is Wee find for The plaintiffe Dept
and Damage Twelfe pounds in good Corrant pay of This Collony and Cost of Court

aprell the 13: 1669 Capt peleg Sanford plaintiffe against henry
underwood in an action of Trespas on the Case damage 200
pound starling pleaded in may verdict of Jury we find for the
Defend Cost of Court not any way Touching the Title of Land
Reheard by the plaintiffe in this Court and the verdict of Jury
is wee find for the Defendant Cost of Court

The Issue is the gennerall Issue

Upon a Rehearing of an action betweene Mr peleg Sanford
and henry underwood The Recorder Joseph Torrey being
Imployed as an atornye in the Case Mr Thomas olnye Juniour
is appoynted by the Court to Sapply his place for Reading of
papers and writting of Testimonyes Whiles the Case is pleading
Mr Thomas hart declared to the Court that in an action betwene
Mr peleg Sanford and henry underwood now upon a Revew
That hee the said Thomas hart Doth Stand to mayntayne the
Case and abide by and performe what shall be detirmined by
verdict of Jury in all Respects and to all Intents and purposes
as fully as the said henry underwood ought to doe himselfe
wherupon the plaintiffe gave way for the said Mr hart to Constitute an atornye in the Case September 27: 1669

Anthony Low plaintiffe against Thomas humphryes mar-
rinor in an action of account for dept damag 200 pound starling an nihil Dicett Entered by the plaintiffe

The verdict of the Jury is

wee find for the plaintiff Damage two hundred pounds starling
and Cost of Court

Robert Gibes and John monrow being Indicted by the grand
Jury and being Called and ther Ind[ic]ments Read before them
pleaded not guiltye and Mr John gard who was bound to procicute the[m] Came into the Court and Did with Draw his proci-

cution desireing the Court to pase it by, and therfore for that Cause and other Reasones appearing to the Court and the said gibes and monrow promising it should be of good use to Cation them for the future They were Cleared by proclamation paying fees.

Page 262

Margrett The Late wife of Robert Collwell being formerly Indicted and being now Called before the Court and asked whether shee were guiltye of adultery or not She did in open Court Confese Shee was guiltye of the acte of adultery The Court Taking notice of her Ingenioues Confestion Doe therfore Remitt halfe the punnishment and halfe the fine Due by the Law for her said offence and accordingly doe Therfore sentance her the said margrett to be but once whipt and that in the Towne of newport on munday this Instant being the first day of november about two of the Clocke at the great gun before Capt morris house with fifteene stripes and to pay alsoe a fine of five pound to the publicke Tresury
Thomas Casse being bound to the peace and alsoe to appeare at this Court and being Called in Court did ther appeare and the Court finding nothinge brought before them wher with to accuse him for breach of his bonds doe pase by his first offence and soe the said Case is Cleared by proclamation paying fees
Ambras Leach being bound to this Court in a bond of fortye pound and being Called in Court did not appeare The Court declare his bonds to be forfitted and the Recorder is advised to Intimate to the said Leach That if hee Can procure favour from the gennerall asembly hee may have his Lebertye Soe to Doe
Sarah flownders being Ingaged to appeare at the Last Court did not appeare the Court Sae Cause to order That Shee should be Summoned in to this Court which was neglected The Court understanding the same Doe order that she shall be summoned in to the next Court

an other grand Jury Impanelled

Mr Edword Smith	Mr Richard Knight
Mr John gould	Mr John peckame
Mr James barker	Mr John pepadye
Mr Robert Stanton	marmeducke Ward
Mr Thomas Clark	Mr Richard Tew
Mr Thomas Burge	Mr Caleb Carr

Benjamin hearden being formerly bound to the Court and being Called did not appeare his bonds were Continued to this Court and being now Called and not appearing The Court declare his bonds to be forfitted and is permitted the Licke previlidge that Leach hath

Thomas Flownders being bound to this Court to procicut against sawakenett and alsoe to the peace and being Called in Court did ther appeare and noe man Coming into Court to accuse him of the breach of his bond hee is Cleared by proclamation paying fees

peter Tollman being bound to the peace and to appeare at this Court and being Called hee appeares and the Court haveing heard the whole that was aleaged against him as the Cause of his being bound soe as to procicutt him any farther hee is Cleared by proclamation paying fees

Edmund Calverlye being Indicted by the grand Jury on a bill siged by Robert Spincke and the said Calverlye presenting his grownds of Exception against the forme of the bill The Court doe adjudge the grownds such that they doe Reject the said bill and the said Calverlye is Cleared by proclamation paying fees

Ther being a bill of Indictment found against georg gardner Ju: and henonye gardner and ther being severall acceptiones against the bill which were owned by John greene agent or atornye as well as by the partyes that were Indicted The Court sees Cause to wave the matter and not to hand any farther proceeds theron

Mr gegory Dexter and william wigingdon being Indicted in the Last Court of Trialles may the 10: 1669 by Mr william harris and were mandamosed in to answer to the said Indictments this Court and being now Called they both appeare and the Court being Informed of the uncomfortablenes that many times doth follow when the puntillioues of the Law are observed in Casses of that nature and hoping that ther will be som way found out to Compose the Defferance by those gentlemen that the gennerall asembly have picked upon to goe to providence to Endevor to Reconcile the two partyes ther that are soe much at variance one with the other and the matters Contayned in these two Indictments very much depending theron The Court are willing to suspend the presant hearing of the matter upon the aforesaid grownds unlese the aforesaid Dexter and Wigington doe prese for ther triall which upon the Courts motion for peace they doe both of them declare they will not nether doe they anyway blame the Court for ther acting and the said Indictment aforesaid for the presant should not be procicutted untill ther be a Retorne from the said five men Cause as aforesd

The Jury on Robert Westcott

william weden	gedian freeborne
peter Easton	John Cowdall
nathanell Dickens	william Cadman
John vahan Ju:	Edword Richmond
Clemant wever	weston Clarke
Thomas Dungen	peter Tollman

Robert westcott being Indicted by the grand Jury may the 10: 1669 and being mandamased to Come to answer the said Indictment did appeare and his Indictment being Read before him he pleaded not guiltye and put him Selfe upon Triall and verdict of the Jury is

we find the Defendant guiltye of the breach of peace but not of felonye

The Sentance of the Court is that the said Robert westcott shall be bound to the good behaviouer in a bond of five pound.

You Leftenant Robert westcott doe owne and acknowlidge your selfe to owe and stand Indepted unto his majestye Charles the second King of England &c: The full and Just Sume of five pound Starling pay able upon all demands

The Condition of the above written obligation is such that if the above bounden Robert westcott shall peacably and Quietly behave himsilfe to all his majestyes Leag people but Espetially to Robert Spencke and his familye and appeare at the next gennerall Court of Triall held for this Collony at newport the first munday next Ensueing the first wensday in may next and then ther appeare. before the Court then this obligation to be voyd and of none Efect otherwise to stand in full force and vertue

Taken in Court

The Jury on will Temberlake and Mary Stockes

william weden	walter Clarke
peter Easton	henry pallmer
nathanell Dickens	nathanell Johnson
william Cadman	Ralph Earll
Edword Richmand	henry bull
Weston Clarke	Thomas fry

William Temberlake being Indicted for Committing adultery with mary stockes being Called in Court and the Indictment Read before him pleads not guiltye and puts himselfe upon Triall by a Jury.

The verdict of the Jury is Guiltye

wheras william Temberlake was Indicted for adultery and found guiltye by the Jury and being Called before the Court and asked what hee had yett to say for himselfe to give the Court grownd to show any favor to him &c: his answer was that hee had sayd all that was with him to say: whereupon the Court Sentanced him to prison to be Kept Close presonor untill munday being the 8 day of november and then to be brought forth to Recive one part of that punnishment that the Law ha[th] provided and the Court hath sentanced him to which as to be whipt at portsmouth with fi[fteen] Stripes and after a weecke Respitt to Recive the Licke at newport and to pay presantly a fi[ne] of Ten pound to the publicke Tresary

Page 263

mary Stockes being Indicted for Committing adultery with william Temberlake and her Indictment being Read before her and being asked whether guilty or not her answer was not guiltye and put her Selfe upon Triall The verdict of the Jury is Guiltye

The Sentance of the Court is

Whereas mary Stockes was Indicted for Committing adultery and found guiltye by the Jury of the aforesd facte The Sentance of the Court is That the aforesaid mary Stockes shall be whipt at portsmouth with fifteene Stripes and after a weeckes Respett to Recive the Licke punnishment at newport and to pay a fine of Ten pound to the publicke Tresury

wheras william Temberlake hath mad an Escape from Justice at presant by voyolent breaking the Collony preson and hee being the principal person in the Transgrestion and the Court Conciveing it necessary to have him if it may bee brought at Last to soffer the Corporall punnishment as well as mary Stockes and ther being hue and Cry gone after him to apprehend him and farther the Court takeing into Consideration the grevious Cryes of mrs mary morris for mercy or some mercy to be Showed to her grandchild (viz) the aforesaid mary Stockes : The Court doe therupon Condescend that the Corporall punnishment of mary stockes shall be suspended for a months time or therabout and then shall at the majestrates Discrestion and appoyntment be once sevearly whipt at newport with fifteen Stripes and shall then haver her Choyce to pay five pound or to be whipt soe againe at portsmou allwayes provided that Shee pay or Cause to be payd into the gennerall Tresury the fine of Ten pounds now presantly or by the Shreefe to witt) James Rogers to be Emediatly taken to gether with the alowance for Takeing the Same by Excicution and that to be done without Delay upon his great perrell

THE JURY ON JOHN CARR

william weden	Clemant wever
peter Easton	John greene Ju.

nathanell Dickens	nathanell Johnson
william Cadman	Ralph Earll
Edword Richmond	henry bull
weston Clarke	walter Clarke

John Carr being Indicted for Contempt of authority and being Called and the Indictment Read before him and being Demanded whether guiltye or not guiltye pleads not guiltye and puts himselfe upon Triall

The verdict of the Jury is Guiltye

John Carr being Indicted for breach of prison and Escape from his Keeper and being Called and the Indictment Read before him and being asked whether guiltye or not guiltye pleads not guiltye and puts himselfe upon Triall)   The verdict of the Jury is guiltye   John Carr being Indicted by henry pallmer for fellony and being Called in Court and the Indictment Read before him and being asked whether guiltye or not guiltye pleads not guiltye and puts himselfe upon Triall The verdict of the Jury is guiltye

John Carr being Convected and found guiltye of breach of peace and breach of prison is sentanced to be Committed to prison till hee find saficient surtyes in two hundred pounds for his good behaviour untill and appearance at the next gennerall Court of Trialles held for this Collony and such surtyes to bring as the governor or Deputye governor, and one asistant with Either of them shall Judge saficient
and being Convicted alsoe of grand Larcany now at this Court is to be whipt sevearly with fifteene stripes and that to be done when the governor Deputye governor and one or more asistants for newport shall appoynt the Exciculion and alsoe is to be Keept in the house of Correction till hee hath payd twelfe Shillings to henry pallmer of newport by way of Restitution for what hee stole from him and haveing mad the said Restitution is not to be Released from prison nevertheless untill hee give such securitye as above said for the good behaviouer

newport octoher 22 : 1669

The Constables of newport to witt John horndell and John

Read Complaining against Job hakens Late Sojournor in newport now of portsmouth that hee the said Job did Contemtiouesly
Refuse Last night at Capt morris house in newport to ayd the
said Constables in watching a man that by a warrant from the
majistrats was to be secured till this morning who was taken
upon suspecstion of a Runaway &c: and alsoe told the Constables hee should not be Keept in that Roome wher hee was
and said plainly hee would not Rise to asist the Constables as
aforesaid wherupon the said Job hakenes being Questioned
before us hee denyed not the premises but with very high Lan-
guage stood to Justifie his said Contempt and being told hee
must gyt suretyes for his good behaviour and to answer for his
Contempt at next Court hee very boldly said that hee should not
bee at the next Court for which his said Contempt hee is Committed to Costadye or prison till hee give securitye for his good
behaviouer till the next Court by two saficient surtyes in a bond
of ten pound or untill the Court take farther order therin before
the Court now sitting be desoulfed

The said Job Hakens making his addrese to the Court by petition dated november 8: 69 for some favour The Court doe grant
that in Case hee Cannot gyt two surtyes for the good abearing
till the next Court and appearance there that then it shall bee in
the power of the majestrats to take one saficient suretye bound
with him, hee sollemly Declaring hee Cannot gyt two to be bound
with him

possunke alias Tom and seaattecke alias Caleb Two Indianes
being Indicted for Lassonye and being Called before the Court
and asked whether they were guiltye of breaching open Thomas
Watermanes Seller and stealing Lyckers out ther &c: or not they
did Ingeneousely Confese they were guiltye and sicksuivelt being
alsoe Indicted for the same fact and Confesed it alsoe The Court
doe Santance the aforesaid Tom and Caleb to pay five shillings
to Thomas waterman Towards satisfaction for the Damage
Done to hime in the aforesaid act of Lassonye and to be whipt
Each of them with fifteene stripes and the said sucksuwatt is
Sentanced to whipe the other two which is the Sentance of the
Court and accordingly Don.

Page 264

The Court being noe way Satisfied what becomes of the fines
and forfitures for severall yeares past that hath ben by Law
Emposed and by the Court of Trialles from time to time past or
Sentenced and ordered to be Recorded and finding the Collonye
much Indepted and nothing in the gennerall Tresury wherwith
to pay the same Therfore the Court sees a necessetyee to order
therin that hencforth ther may bee a Remedye to that Default
and to that End doe order and Require the gennerall Recorder
to Draw forst a List of all fines that are by sentance of the
Court adjudged to be Levied &c : and to send the said Lest with
a Coppie of this order to the gennerall Tresurer of the Collony
That hee may therby be in a Capassitye to Call upon the gen
Sargent to gather the said fines and bring them in unto the said
Tresurer as alsoe the Recorder is to Looke over the Records
and to take out a List of all the fines and forfiturs hath ben
Recorded for all those yeares since Mr John Coggeshall now
Tresurer was Last Chosen and yearly soe Continued in that
office That hee may therby be able to Inquire into and Call the
said sargant to give him an account what therof hath ben Taken
and how Disposed of That soe the Tresury may be furnished
wherwith to Defray the Collonyes depts and this to be don with
all Expidition by the Recorder.

Suwaganitt The Indian being bound to appeare and answer
at Court and the two Sachins Called mosup and nenecraft being
bound with him for his appearance accordingly The said suwaganitt being Called apeared not and therfore the Court doe
adjudge and Declare ther bonds are forfitted being to the value
of one hundred pound But the Court sitting againe on munday
november 8th haveing somethinge unfineshed of other Concearnes and Sawaganitt presenting him selfe to the Court and
the Jury being gone by Leave of the Court and Thomas Flounders Dischaiged of his bond to procicutt at this Court and soe
Court in noe Capassitye to heare the matter as to a Triall The
Court haveing upon his the said Sawaganitt now appearing
when Called declared the bonds to be forfitted as abovesaid It
is now Therfore ordered and declared That Mosup and nene-

craft ought not to stand Longer Bound but seeing the principall
partye is heare hee ought to be Imprisoned and the said mosup
and nenicraft are Discharged of ther bonds and the said Sawaganitt is Committed to prison ther to Remaine untill hee doe procure Suficiant surtyes in the sume of one hundred pounds Starlinge that hee shall Satisfie Thomas Flownders before the next
Court of Trialles and that hee shall behave him selfe well and
orderly in mene Time and appeare at the said next Court to
answer for his misdemenure &c: as alsoe to abide The Courts
award for the Satisfaction of the said flownders &c: in Case it
be not done Efectually in meane time as aforesaid.

Amos westcott Chosen Jury man by the Toune of warwicke
and not appereing is fined Twentye Shillings
Benjamin Barton and John warner Chosen to be on the Jury
of Trialles and not appearing are fined Twentye shillings apeace
John Badcocke being Chosen to be on the Jury of Triall and not
appearing is by the Court fined Twentye shillings

Page 271

The proceeds of the Court of Trialles may the ninth 1670
Mr Benedict Arnold governor
Mr nicholas Easton Deputye governor
Capt John Cranston asistant
Mr John Coggshall asistant
Mr John Easton asistant
Mr William Carpender asistant
Mr Roger Williams asistant
Mr Thomas olnye asistant
Mr william Baulston asistant
Mr John Trip asistant
Capt John greene asistant
Mr James Greene asistant
Joseph Torrey Recorder
Mr James Rogers gennerall sargant
Mr John Coggeshall gennerall Tresurer
Mr John Sanford gen atornye

The grand Jury

Mr Richard Tew	Mr andrew harris
Mr John pecham Sen	Mr Lathem Clarke
Mr Thomas Clarke	Mr william wilboure
Mr Larrance Turner	Mr hugh persones
Mr nathanell Dickens	Mr John badcocke
Mr Thomas harris Ju	Mr william almye

An action of unjust Detaynure Entered September the 18: 1669: by Mr William almye against Mr william baulstone Tresurer of the Toune of portsmouth and in the behalfe of the towne Defendant Damage five hundred pound Demured to this Cour[t] and now pleaded

The verdict of the Jury   The Issue being not guiltye wee find for the Defendant Cost of Court

The Jury peter Easton george hallsell weston Clarke Thomas ward Samuell hubberd Thomas hopkens Richard Knight Richard baily henry bull John badcocke nathanell Dickens Jefery Champ[lin]

Page 272

Wheras Job hakens was Indicted by the Atornye gennerall for misbehavior &c: and being Called before the Court and his Indictment Read before him and asked whether guiltye or not guiltye he Confesed him Selfe guiltye and Referes himselfe to the Court   The Court Taking notice of his willing Submitting himselfe to the Court as alsoe Considering that in october Last before the aforesaid offence was Committed hee did service by order in beating the drome &c: The Court doe acquitt the Said Job hakens from his bond without farther penaltye upon his solleme promise of his good behaviouer for the future hee paying Fees

Wheras Mr Samuell gorton Mr John weeckes Sen: and Mr Edmund Calverlye were arested in Three actiones Commenced by Mr John Easton gen atornye in the Collonyes name &c: and the Court Consedering the Late gen asemblyes act as to an awditt that is to pase on all such Casses as the actiones Concearne The Court sees Cause that the actiones be withdrane

Wheras Thomas Jennings of portsmouth was bound in a bond of Twentye pound Starling to procicut a Charge of Saspision of fellony against Thomas Durffe of portsmouth &c: and the said Jennings not being furnished sutable at presant to procicute the same Desires hee may withdraw the procicution and be Cleare of his bond which Request the Court grants

Sarah Greene alias Flounders being mandamas to appeare to answer for fornication and her father John Greene being Called to Informe the Court why his Daster did not appeare And doth say that it is not out of Contempt to the Court but by Reson of shortnes of time and multiplisitye of busines &c and the said John Greene on his Dasters behalfe Doth Confese that shee is guilty of fornication and Doth promise to answer the Law in that Case provided
on the Case of Sarah greene alias Sarah flounders John greene her father Came before the Court and did Ingage that hee would pay unto the Tresurrer fortye shillings in Corrant pay of the Collony as the Law Requires for fornication

THE JURY ON JOHN COTTRELL &C

peter Easton	william wilbour
Jarod borne	Latham Clarke
samuell hubberd	hugh persones
henry bull	John badcocke
georg halsell	James badcocke
Jefery Champian	John peckam

John Cottrell, gersham Cottrell and John medbery being Indicted by Richard Knight and being Called before the Court and ther Indictment Read before them and asked whether guiltye or not guilty plead not guiltye and put them selfes upon Triall

The verditt of the Jury not guilty They are Cleared by proclamat- paying fees

ON SUBALL PAYNTER

peter Easton	william wilbour
Jarod borne	Latham Clarke
Samuell hubberd	hugh persones

henry bull	John badcocke
george halsell	John greene
Jeffey Champian	James badcocke

Shuball paynter being Indicted for breach of peace and being Called before the Court and his Indictment Read before him and asked whether he were guiltye or not guiltye pleads not guiltye and puts himselfe upon Triall the verditt of the Jury is not guiltye and was Cleared by proclamation paying fees

Elizabeth hopkins being bound to this Court and being Indicted for Committing fornication with william gregory and being Called and her Indictment Read before her and being asked whether guiltye or not guiltye she Confeseth her selfe guiltye and her father Thomas hopkins Doth Engage to pay fortye shillings to the gen Tresurer For her facts The Court adjudgeth she is free from her bond as is freeed by proclamation paying fees

THE JURY ON WILL: GREGORY

peter Easton	John greene
Jarod borne	Thomas hart
henry bull	John Rogers
Jefery Champion	weston Clarke
James badcocke	Ed Richmon
John pecham Ju:	Tho: mumford

William gregory being Indicted for Committing fornication with Elizabeth hopkins and his Indictment Read before him and asked whether guiltye or not guiltye plead not guiltye and puts himselfe upon Triall The verditt of the Jury is Guilty

The Judgment of the Court is that hee pay a fine of fortye shilling or be whipt

Mr Samuell gorton Ju: Chosen to serve on the grand Jury and not appearing is fined 20s

Mr Elizah Collines Chosen by the towne of warwicke to serve on the grand Jury and not appearing is fined 20s

Ensigne John Blise and Mr Edword Smith Chosen by the Towne of newport to serve on the Jury of Trialles and not appearing are fined 20s shilling apeece Samuell bennett of providence for not atending the Jury as Chosen to fined 20s

Edword Smith of providence Chosen by the Towne to serve on
the Jury of Triars and not appearing is fined Twentye shillings

Page 277

The proceeds of The Court of Triall october the 19: 1670
Mr Benidict Arnold governor
Mr nicholas Easton Deputye governor
Capt John Cranston asistant
Mr John Cogshall asistant
Mr John Easton asistant
Mr william Carpenter asistant
Mr Roger williams asistant
Mr Thomas olnye asistant
Mr william Baulston
Mr John Trip asistant
Capt John greene asistant
Mr James greene asistant
Joseph Torrey gen Recorder
Mr James Rogers gen Sargant
Mr John Coggshall Tresurer
Mr John Sanford gen atornye

Grand Jury

Mr John Sailes	Left Edmund Calverlye
Mr John Cowdall	Mr william Case
Mr nathanell Dickes	Mr Jarod borne
Mr John gould	Mr John odlin
Mr John pechan	Mr Edword Roberson
Left frances brayton	Mr Thomas Rogers

Jury on Mr Mr almie aganst Mr baulston

peter Easton	Weston Clarke
Edword Greenman	Thomas mamford
John greene	Steven mumford
John gorton	Robert Tayler
Edward marshall	John Read
william Rogers	James blower

Wheras ther was an action of unjust detaynure Entered by Mr william almye against Mr william baulston Tresurer of the Towne of portsmouth and in the behalfe of the Towne of portsmouth defendant which action beares date september the 18 1669: demured by the defendant on october and pleaded in the Court may the ninth 1670 and the verditt was wee find for the defendant Cost of Court and Reheard in this Court and the verditt of the Jury is wee find for the defendant Cost of Court.

Judgment granted by the Court

Wheras ther was an action Commenced by henry greene against Ralph Cowland and pleaded before the Court and put to the Jury and before ther was an acteplation of the verditt in Court the partyes Concarned did agree to both ther Satisfaction wherupon The Court doe order that the foreman and Jury doe delever in the papers that were delevered to them to the Recorder and soe thy are discharged from action

Wheras ther was a sute Commenced and by the Court admitted by Joseph Card of newport against william Case of the Same Toune for wast made upon the farme of the said Card and the said action being Called in Court The said action was by Joynt Consent Committed to arbitration provided it were Ended by Saterday on which day both partyes being Called Into Court and were asked whether they were agreed or whether the matter most come to Court to which thy both answered ther was an award given by the arbitrators (to witt) Edward Richmond and Richard bayly which They were Resoulfed to stand to and abide.

Wheras Thomas star was bound in a bond of Twentye pound That Samuell Eldred Seni- should appeare in this Court to answer to such Charges as shall be charged against him in the present Court and hee haveing brought the said Eldred into Court the said Thomas Starr is freed from his aforesaid bond John Frinke of stowingtoune being Indicted for Excercising athority within this Jurisdiction not being Legally Called therto and being Called and his Indictment Read before him and asked whether guiltye or not guiltye plead not guiltye and puts himselfe upon Triall of god and the Country

The Juryes verditt guiltye   The Court Judgment granted

Wheras Mr John Frinke was bound to appeare in this presant Court and haveing heare appeared and having Traversed his Indictment and found guiltye by the Jury &c and haveing been againe Called before the Court and haveing Engaged himselfe that hee will not meddle in the Excercise of any office in this Jurisdiction without being duely Called therto by this Collony or the freemen therof hee the said John frinke is Discharged from any farther atendance on this Court

John Cole of narragansitt being Indicted and being Called before the Court and his Indictment Read before him and being asked whether guiltye or not giultye to which hee answers hee did not denye any thing of the Charge

The Judgment of the Court is that hee be bound in a bond of good behaviouer untill the next Court &c:

Page 278

You John Cole Living in the narragansitt Country or Kings province doe Recognise unto his majestye Charles the second King of England scotland france and Ireland &c: in the sume of fiftye pound starling payable to Mr John Coggshall Tresurer or his sureties upon all demands and this to be Levied on your goods and Chattles

The Condition of this obligation is such that if the above boundden John Cole shall apeare personally at the next Court of Trialles to be holden for the Collony at newport the first munday next Ensueing the first wensday in may next and not to Depart without the Leave of the Court and in the meane Time to bee of a good and peacable behaviouer Towards all his majestyes Leige people as alsoe to for beare to Excercise authoritye within the Limitts of this Jurisdiction or Kings province not being Lawfully Called therunto as being apart of the said good behaviouer upon due observation of the premises this obligation to be voyd but otherwise to stand in full force and vertue

owned in Court by the above said John Cole that hee will appeare and that hee will for beare to Excersice authority in the meane time by the authoritye of Conetticott

Samuell Eldred Sen: being Indicted for Excercising authority in this jurisdiction which Indictment being Read before him and asked whether guiltye or not guiltye to which hee plead not guiltye and upon much debate the Court doth sentance him to be bound to appeare at next Court and in meane time to be of good behaviour &c

which bond followes

You Samuell Eldrid Living in the narragansitt Country or Kings province doe Recognize unto his majestye Charles the second King of England scotland france and Ireland &c: in the sume of fiftye pound starling payable to Mr John Coggshall Tresurer or his successors upon all demands and this to be Levied on your goods or Chattles The Condition of this obligation is such that if the above bounden Samuell Eldrid shall appeare personally at the next Court of Trialles to be holden for this Collony at newport the first munday next Ensueing the first wensday in may next and not to depart without the Leave of the Court and in the meane time to be of agood and peacable behaviouer Towards all his majestyes Leige people as alsoe to forbeare to Exercise authority within the Limitts of This Jurisdiction or Kings province not being Lawfully Called ther unto as being apart of the said good behaviour upon due observation of the premises This obligation to be voýd but otherwise to stand in full forse and vertue

THE JURY ON THOMAS FLOUNDERS

william Smiton	Edword marshall
peter Easton	Richard Knight
John pepodye	Thomas ward
Thomas Cornall	Left John albro
John almye	Ralph Earll
John gorton	george Layton

Thomas Flounders being Indicted for felonioues murdering walter house Inhabetant in the Kings province on the 11 day of July 1670 by severall strockes or blowers &c and being Called before the Court and his Indictment Read before him and being asked whether guilty or not guiltye plead not guiltye and puts himselfe upon the Triall of god and the Country Juryes verdict guiltye of manslaughter

Thomas Flounders alias Flonders being Indicted for felonioues murdering walter house and having put himselfe upon the Trialles of god and the Country and the verditt of the Jury is guiltye of man slaughter The Judgment of the Court is unanimously That hee suffer death as the Law hath provided in Such Casses which is to be hanged untill his body be dead which sentance is to be Excicuted on wensday being the 2 Day of november betweene the owre of nine in the morning and two in the afternone

THE JURY ON WILL HAKENS INDICTMENT

peter Easton	william Rogers
Edword greenman	nicolas Easton Ju:
John greene	steven mumford
weston Clarke	Edward marshall
Robert Tayler	Thomas brockes
John Read	steven wilcoxes

William hakens of providence sen: being Indicted for grand Larcanye by feloniouesly Taking a horse of Coller Roane belonging to John gorton of warwicke &c and being Called before the Court and his Indictment Read before him and asked whether guilty or not guiltye pleads not guiltye and puts himselfe upon Triall of god and the Country

The verditt of the Jury is not guiltye

Upon the verditt Judgment granted that he is Cleared by proclamation paying fees

may the 22: 1670 an action of Dept Entered by James Rogers, gen sargant against John Carr Late presoner in the preson in newport

a nihil Dicett Taken in Court   The verditt of the Jury wee find for the plaintiff Damage and Cost of Court Ten pounds

JURY ON JAMES ROGERS JOHN CARR AND SAM REAPE AND

ROBERT WESTCOTT

peter Easton	Robert Tayler
John greene	John Read
John gorton	James blower

Edword marshall	william Rogers
weston Clarke	nicolas Easton
Thomas mumford	Edword greenman

november the 30: 1669: an action of dept Entered by Samuell Reape against Robert westcott damage 20 pound starling The verdict of the Jury

    wee find for the plaintiffe seven pound Ten Shillings damage and Cost of Court

Judgment granted

march the Tenth 1669: or 70 an action of the Case for none performance of Conven. Entered by Mr John Sanford plain·· tiffe against Capt Randall houldon of the Toune of warwicke defendant damage one hundred and Twentye pound starling

    The Issue Joyned not guiltye The Juryes verdict

        wee find for the defendant Cost of Court

Judgment granted by the Court

THE JURY ON THE CASE

peter Easton	Thomas mumford
Edword greeman	Robert Tayler
John greene	John Read
John gorton	James blower
Edword marshall	william Rogers
weston Clarke	nicolas Easton

Page 279 THE JURY ON THE CASE OF THOMAS HART AGAINST MARKE REDLYE

peter Easton	weston Clarke
Edword greenman	Thomas mumford
John greene	steven mumford
John gorton	Robert Tayler
Edword marshall	John Read
william Rogers	James blower

July the 5: 1670 an action of the Case for none performance of a bill of Loading Entered by Mr Thomas hart of newport against marke Redlye marriner and master of the Kach hopwell damage forty pound starling

The Issue Joyned not guiltye The verditt of the Jury is wee find for the Defendant Cost of Court

Reheard by the Plaintiffe

To mr John porter at petaquamscott in the King province These present with Sped

Mr John porter wheras you were summonsed by the governor and severall asistan posotively to appeare personally at this gen Court of Trialles to give Evidence for the King Concearning the death of walter house &c but you not obaying the sommones in Comminge accordingly but sending in your Testimony written in such words as Renders your former and Later declaration to Clash one against the other which to Lett pose as Testimony in soe high Concearne will Render the Court in a dangerous Condition and the matter Intracate beyond our power to Cleare it but it may bee you have not Explained your selfe as you would. or we Cannot understand it Therfore yo[u] are in his majestyes name promptoryly Required without delay Laying aside all Excuses Emmediatly upon sight hearof to Repaire with all possable Expedition unto this Court to give in your Testamony personally in open Court on the premised Case hear of you may not fayle as you will answer the Contrary at your great perrell

Dated at the gen Court of Trialles held at newport october 19: 1670 Signed by order of the said Court

Joseph Torrey gennerall Recorder

To mr Edword Richmond Constituted high Constable by Special order in this presant occation These greeting

You are by vertue hearof Required in his majestyes name Charles the second King of England Scotlant france and Ireland &c to Require you to take saficiant ayd with you as alsoe to prese a saficiant boat and with it and them to goe to petaquamiscott to the house of Mr John porter and to bring him to witt the said porter before this presant Court now sitting in newport on Thirsday being the 27: of this Insta october by Eight of the Clocke in the morning then and there to answer to suc[h] Things as shall be Required of him hearof you may not fayle at your perrell

Dated in the Court october 25 : 1670   by order of the Court
                    Joseph Torrey gen Recorder
ordered that Mr Edword Richmond who is Commistionated to goe to petaquamsc[ott] shall have Thirtye shillings for his paynes and Travill in that voyge besids boat hyre and ayd ordered that the Recorder shall grant forth a writt of Restitution Concernin[g] the horse that william hakens was Indicted for which is to be to Mr. Joh[n] Throgmorton from whome hee was Taken

Wheras ther was a sute Commenced by John Knowles of warwicke against an Indian Called wawenauckshott it is Refered to the gennerall asembly to order therin

andrew harris Chosen a grand Jury man by the Toune of providence and not appearing is fined Twentye shillings

Ensigne Lott strange Chosen A Jury man by the Towne of portsmouth and not appearing was fined Twentye Shillings Caleb arnold Chosen by the Toune of portsmouth to serve on the grand Jury and not appearing was fined Twentye Shillings Except it appears he was not warned

Mr Richard Carder Chosen by the Toune of warwicke to serve on the grand Jury and not appearing was fined Twentye shillings John Lewes Chosen by the Toune of westerlye to serve on the grand Jury and not appearing was fined Twentye Shillings

Edword Smith Chosen (to serve on the Jury of Triares) by the Toune of newport and not appearing was fined Twentye Shillengs

John whippell Seni and John whippell Ju : Chosen by the Towne of providence to serve on the Jury of Triares and not appearing are fined Twenty shillings apeece

INDEX